Pupil's Book **3**

ICT InteraCT
for KS3

Pupil's Book **3**

ICT InteraCT
for KS3

Bob Reeves
Consultant: Alan Plumpton

The Publishers would like to thank the following for permission to reproduce copyright material:

Photo credits: p.5 *tl* © Steve Chenn/Corbis, *tr* Andy Crawford and Dave King/Dorling Kindersley/Getty Images, *cl* © Yevgen Timashov/Alamy; **p.64** Sylvain Grandadam/Robert Harding Travel/Photolibrary Group; **p.65** *c* Martin Lee/Rex Features; **p.66** *tl* © Ilian Studio/Alamy, *tr* © Joe Tree/Alamy, *cl* The logo is a registered trademark of Daimler AG and is reproduced with the kind permission of Daimler AG/Photo © Mediacolor's/Alamy, *cr* © 2002–2008 Sony Computer Entertainment Inc., All Rights Reserved, *bl* Kellogg's, *bc* Kellogg's/ Photo © Mediablitzimages (UK) Limited/Alamy, *br* Kellogg's; **p.76** © Simon Jarratt/Corbis; **p.78** *t* © Mira/Alamy, *b* © VIEW Pictures Ltd/Alamy; **p.79** *b* ITV/Rex Features; **p.80** *t* © Jupiter Images/Comstock Images/Alamy, *b* © Jose Goitia/Corbis; **p.81** *t* © Deepak Buddhiraja/India Picture/Corbis, *b* © Hulton-Deutsch Collection/Corbis; **p.82** *t* Jakub Mosur /AP Photo/PA Photos; **p.83** *t* © Howard Pyle/zefa/Corbis, *b* Marc Volk/fStop/Photolibrary Group; **p.84** *t* © Geogphotos/Alamy, *b* Gregor Schuster/Photonica/Getty Images; **p.85** *t* © Travelshots.com/Alamy, *b* © Lucy P/Alamy.

Acknowledgements: p.6 *t* IBM, *c* BBC Online, *b* Teach Yourself, Hodder Education; **p.47** MySpace; **p.48** Facebook; **p.49** BBC Online; **p.65** *tl* Xbox.com, *tr* The Internet Encyclopaedia of Philosophy; **p.74** Wikipedia.

t=top, *b*=bottom, *l*=left, *r*=right, *c*=centre

Microsoft product screenshots reprinted by permission of Microsoft Corporation. Microsoft and Windows are trademarks of Microsoft Corporation.

Every effort has been made to trace all copyright holders, but if any have been inadvertently overlooked the Publishers will be pleased to make the necessary arrangements at the first opportunity.

Although every effort has been made to ensure that website addresses are correct at time of going to press, Hodder Education cannot be held responsible for the content of any website mentioned in this book. It is sometimes possible to find a relocated web page by typing in the address of the home page for a website in the URL window of your browser.

Hachette's policy is to use papers that are natural, renewable and recyclable products and made from wood grown in sustainable forests. The logging and manufacturing processes are expected to conform to the environmental regulations of the country of origin.

Orders: please contact Hachette UK Distribution,
Hely Hutchinson Centre, Milton Road,
Didcot, Oxfordshire, OX11 7HH. Telephone: +44 (0)1235 827827.
Email education@hachette.co.uk
Lines are open from 9 a.m. to 5 p.m., Monday to Friday.
You can also order through our website:
www.hoddereducation.com

Microsoft and Windows are trademarks of Microsoft Corporation.

© Bob Reeves 2008
First published in 2008 by
Hodder Education,
a member of the Hachette Livre UK Group,
338 Euston Road,
London NW1 3BH.

Impression number   17
Year   2023

Cover photo Pixland/Jupiter Images
Illustrations by Tony Jones/Art Construction and Magic Software Pvt. Ltd.
Typeset in 13.5/15pt ITC Officina Sans by Stephen Rowling/Springworks
Printed by CPI Group (UK) Ltd, Croydon CR0 4YY

A catalogue record for this title is available from the British Library

ISBN: 978 0340 940 990

CONTENTS

INTRODUCTION

Welcome to ICT InteraCT Book 3. The book has eight main *modules*:

> Module 1 Podcasting
> Module 2 Computer games
> Module 3 Shape recognition
> Module 4 Creating a social networking website
> Module 5 Crime solving
> Module 6 Working with graphics
> Module 7 Creating a wiki
> Module 8 Security systems

Most of the modules have additional Skills Tutorials spreads, where you can learn a related ICT skill.

There is a website to support this course, which contains an electronic copy of the book and lots of other resources that you'll need to boost your knowledge and understanding of ICT, and to develop your practical skills. Your teacher will show you the electronic version of the book and you will find that its layout looks exactly the same as the printed pages. The electronic version works a bit like a web page because it has lots of links in it that will open up other resources.

You will notice that the pages have various icons on them. On the electronic version of the book, these icons will link you to the other resources. Before you get started, it is worth having a quick look at how the pages are laid out and what each of the icons mean.

Here is a list of the icons you will come across in this book:

 Written Tasks

 Practical Tasks

 Skills Tutorials

Practical Tasks: These are tasks where you will be asked to do something on the computer.

Skills Tutorials: These are 'how to' guides that will show you how to do things on the computer.

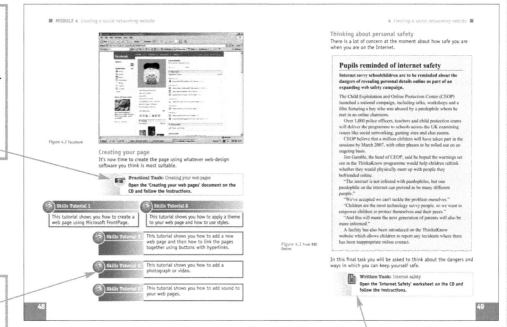

Written Tasks: These are tasks that you don't need a computer for. Your teacher might ask you to do these for homework, or you might do them if you have a lesson when you are not in the computer room.

Challenges

These challenges are for pupils who have already completed the 8 main modules in this book. They are designed to be very different from the main tasks in Modules 1 to 8. You should not attempt them until your teacher tells you to.

The idea of the challenges is to give you the chance to really show off your ICT capability. The challenges are deliberately open-ended so that you can tackle them in whatever way you think is suitable.

For example, Challenge 4 asks you to create a soap opera. You are not told exactly how to do this because we want you to decide for yourself how you want to do it. For example, you may work on your own, in a pair or a group. You may choose to create a sound recording or video recording, or create a storyboard using animations or photographs. You may think of a completely new way of creating a soap opera and do that!

You need to discuss how you are going to tackle each challenge with your teacher and how much time you need to do it. After that it is over to you to get the challenge finished using all the skills and knowledge that you have learnt.

Podcasting

In this module you will use a range of ICT skills and knowledge to:

> **Research a topic**
> **Plan and write an appropriate script for a podcast**
> **Record and edit a podcast that is suitable for a particular audience**
> **Review other people's podcasts and provide feedback**
> **Make changes to your own podcast based on feedback**

Introduction

In this module you will be using ICT to create your own podcast. A podcast is a sound or video file that is made available on the Internet. Podcasts can be created by anyone and they can cover any topic. They can be viewed or listened to using a computer or any type of handheld device including mp3 players, PDAs and mobile phones. Here are just a few examples of what podcasts can be used for:

> Keeping up to date with the news headlines.
> Listening to edited highlights of radio programmes.
> Watching or listening to a performance by a comedian.
> Finding out about the latest computer and technology issues.
> Learning a foreign language.

What makes podcasts different is that they are usually made available as a series of ongoing episodes, rather than just a one-off. People can subscribe to the podcasts, which means that they get the latest episode as soon as it is made available on the Internet.

Getting started

To make your own podcasts you need some basic equipment and software.

> **Digital camera**: If you want to create a video podcast then you will need a camera of some sort. You could use a webcam although you will be limited to what you can do as the camera is in a fixed position. A digital video camera gives you more options.

Figure 1.1 Webcam

Figure 1.2 Digital video camera

> **Microphone**: If you want to create any audio you will need a microphone. Most computers, webcams and digital video cameras have microphones built in.
> **Software**: You will need software to record and then edit your podcast. There is a lot to choose from. Some of it is free and some of it is very expensive. We have used Audacity, which is free and can be used for audio, and Movie Maker, which comes as part of Windows and can be used to video.

Figure 1.3 Microphone

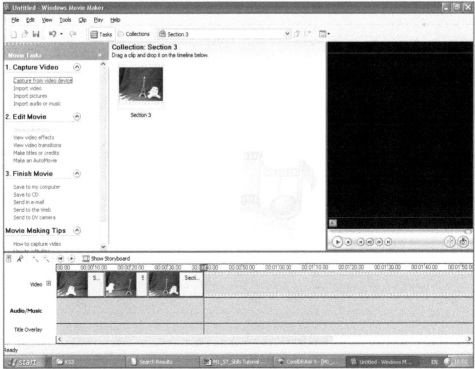

Figure 1.4 Windows Movie Maker

Examples of podcasts

Below are some still images from typical podcasts you might find.

Figure 1.5 Finding out about the latest computer and technology issues at IBM Online

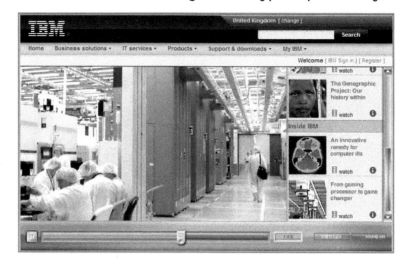

Figure 1.6 Keeping up to date with the news headlines at BBC Online

Figure 1.7 Learning a foreign language with the Teach Yourself One-day French podcast

Creating your own podcast

It's now time for you to create your own podcast. Depending on the equipment and software available in your school, you may be creating a sound-only or a video podcast.

 **Skills Tutorial 1** — This tutorial shows you how to create a sound-only podcast using Audacity software.

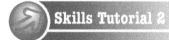 **Skills Tutorial 2** — This tutorial shows you how to create a video podcast using Windows Movie Maker software.

A podcast is way of communicating information. Like any other form of communication you need to think about the audience and purpose. For example, a comedian who releases a podcast every week does so to entertain people.

 Practical Task: Planning a podcast

Think of your podcast as if it were a radio or TV programme. You need to plan it, research it and write a script. Open the 'Planning a podcast' worksheet on the website and follow the instructions.

 Practical Task: Creating a podcast

You now need to record it and edit it into an episode that's worth listening to or watching. Open the 'Creating a podcast' worksheet on the website and follow the instructions.

 Practical Task: Reviewing a podcast

Once you have created it, you need to ask others for their comments and feedback. You may want to make changes to the original, or create a new podcast to respond to the feedback. Open the 'Reviewing a podcast' worksheet on the website and follow the instructions.

1 | SKILLS TUTORIAL 1

This tutorial will show you how to record and edit sound using Audacity software. Audacity is available free from the Internet and has a number of useful features, such as the ability to edit what you have recorded and the ability to overlay soundtracks on top of each other. For example, you could record a spoken voice and then put some music in the background.

Recording sound using Audacity

First load the Audacity software.

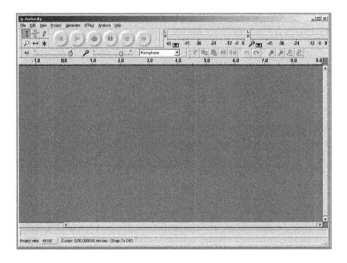

Figure 1.8 Audacity

The main controls are at the top of the screen. Standard media player controls are used here so you are probably familiar with them already. To record, click on the red circle.

Figure 1.9 The main controls

To record, you must make sure that you have a microphone. There may be one built in to your computer, or you can use a plug-in microphone. Some headsets and webcams have built-in microphones.

As you speak you will see the sound wave moving, as shown below, which gives you an idea of the volume. You may need to experiment with this to get the right distance from the microphone.

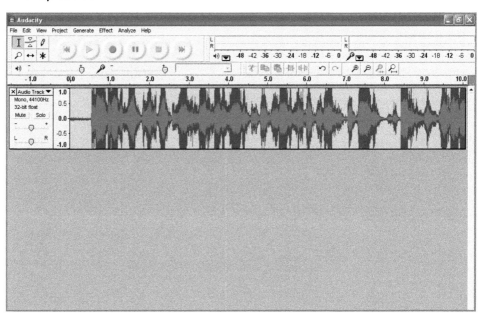

Figure 1.10 Sound wave

When you have finished, press the yellow rectangle to stop the recording.

You can now save the sound file:

- Click 'File'.
- Click on 'Save project'.

The standard setting is to save as an aup file, which is a format specific to the Audacity software, but you can also save as a wav or mp3 file by selecting the appropriate option in the 'File' menu. The advantage of saving as mp3 or wav is that the sound file you have made can easily be transferred onto a handheld device such as an mp3 player or mobile phone.

To listen to what you have recorded:

- Click on 'File' and 'Open' and find the file you want to listen to.
- Click on the 'Play' button and you should now be able to hear your sound file.

Editing sound using Audacity

The advantage of using Audacity software is that you can edit the sound later on so, if you make a mistake, you can delete it and just re-record the sentence where you went wrong.

If you look at the example below, you can see that there is a period of about three seconds at the beginning before the sound starts to play. This could be removed.

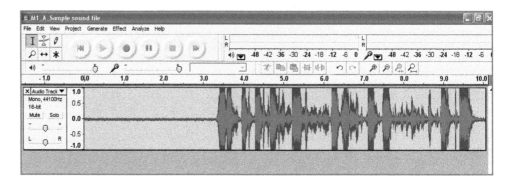

Figure 1.11 Clip that needs editing

Figure 1.11 Clip that needs editing

To do this, click on the sound wave where you want to delete. In this case we have clicked just after three seconds, where the main sound wave starts, just after the flat part of the wave.

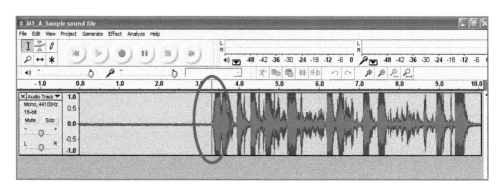

Figure 1.12 Editing a sound wave

A small hand will be displayed on the screen.

● Drag this across to the beginning of the sound wave; it will highlight as you move the mouse across.
● Select 'Edit' and then 'Delete'.

This will remove the part of the sound wave that was the period of silence before the actual recording.

You can delete any part of the recording using this method. For example, if there was a long pause, or a background noise, you could make a note of when this happens by looking at the seconds across the top, and then delete that bit.

You can also import other sound files and lay tracks on top of each other. This means that you could have music as a backing track, for example, while you talk over the top.

To do this:

● Select 'Project'.
● Select 'New audio track'.

A new line will now be displayed where you can record another track to be played at the same time as your original track.

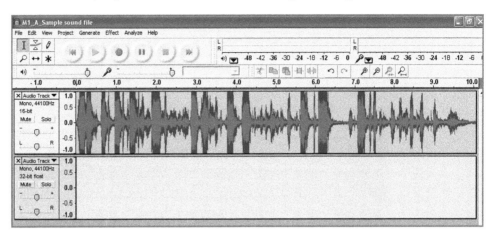

Figure 1.13 Importing a new audio file

You can record another track at this point or import other sound files, for example a music track:

● Select 'Project'.
● Select 'Import audio'.
● Select the sound file that you want to import: it will appear as a new line or lines in the main window.

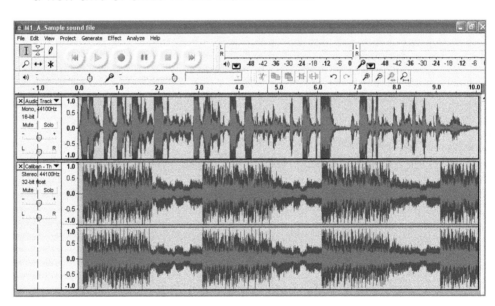

Figure 1.14 Multiple audio tracks

You can now use the editing techniques described earlier to make sure that the two tracks start and end at the right time. For example, you might want to have some music playing as an introduction and then have a voice talking over the top. At the end you might want to finish the music and talking at the same time, or have the music playing after the talking has finished.

1| SKILLS TUTORIAL 2

This tutorial will show you how to record and edit video using Windows Movie Maker software. Movie Maker comes as part of Windows XP and Windows Vista. This tutorial uses the Windows XP version. Movie Maker has a number of useful features, such as the ability to edit what you have recorded, and the ability to add audio tracks and titles to make your video look like a professional movie or video podcast.

Recording video and sound using Movie Maker

Load the Movie Maker software. The main window looks like this:

This part of the screen shows you still images of each section of video that you have captured. Movie Maker automatically splits videos up into separate sections to make it easier to edit it later on.

This part of the screen gives you additional help on the three main processes of recording your movie, editing it and then saving it in a suitable format.

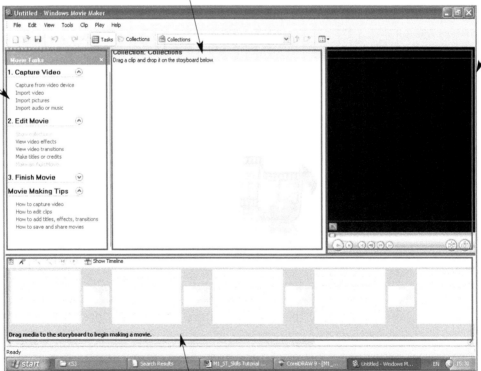

This part of the screen will play the video that you have captured. Notice the usual media player controls for playing, pausing and stopping the video.

This part of the screen shows you each section of the video. You can put different parts of the video together here and add special effects if you want to. This is called the timeline.

Figure 1.15 Movie Maker

To record, you must have a camera of some sort. Ideally this will be a digital camcorder. Alternatively you can use a webcam, although this limits what you can video as it is attached to the computer. You also need a built-in microphone to capture sound.

It is possible to import videos that other people have made and edit them in Movie Maker, but we will concentrate on making our own.

If you are using a digital camcorder you will need to transfer the movie file onto the computer and then select 'Import video'. To record a movie using a webcam:

- Click on 'Capture from video device'.
- On the next screen it will show you the settings for any cameras that are plugged into the computer. Click 'Next'.
- You now need to choose a suitable folder and give your video a name.

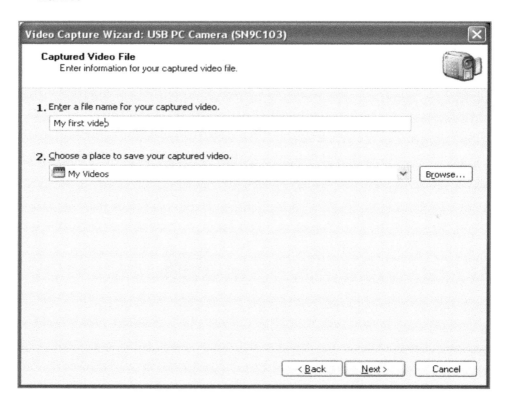

Figure 1.16 Recording a movie using a webcam

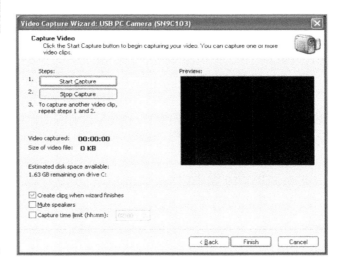

Figure 1.17 Video capture

- You will now see another screen where you can choose the quality of video that you want. Choose the highest possible and click 'Next'.
- You will now see the screen where you can capture the video. Click 'Finish' to end the video capture.

Movie Maker automatically splits your movie up into parts. If your movie is quite short then you will only see one part, as shown below. If you video is quite long, you will see a number of still images that show you each part. This is a bit like the chapter selection option you get on DVD video menus.

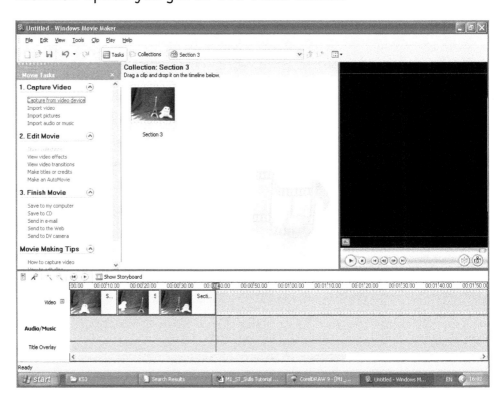

Figure 1.18 Movie with only one part

You can now drag and drop each part of the video into the timeline across the bottom of the screen. If there are sections that you don't want to use, don't put them on the timeline.

The image above shows three separate movies that have been put together to create a longer movie. To add in different movies:

- Select 'File'.
- Select 'Import to selections'.
- Then drag and drop it into the timeline.

To save at any stage:

- Click on 'File'.
- Select 'Save project' and give it a name: this saves the video as it appears in the timeline.

Notice that it is saved as a Movie Maker file with an MSWMM suffix. We can change this to a suitable format such as mp3 later on.

To play the video, drag the pointer on the timeline to the beginning and then click the play icon on the media player (where you can see the large image of the movie).

Editing video and sound using Movie Maker

At this stage you might decide to re-record certain parts of the movie, or delete certain scenes. It is probably easier to record your movie in small sections so that, if anything goes wrong, you can re-record that section. You can use the timeline to add and remove sections of the movie or slot new sections in.
To delete a section of video:

- Highlight the section that you want to delete and click 'Edit' and 'Delete'.

To add a section of video:

- Record the section as described before.
- Drag the new section into the timeline at the point that you want it to appear.

There are a number of different effects that you can add to the movie and you are encouraged to experiment with these. They can all be added in the same way:

- Click on 'Tools' and select 'Video effects'.
- Drag the effect onto the section of video that you want it on in the timeline.
- Play the video to see if you like the effect.
- You can add effects and transitions to any section of the video in this way.
- You can also add several effects to the same section of video.

If you want to remove any of the effects:

- Right-click on the section of video that contains the effect.
- Select 'Video effects'.
- You can now add or remove the effects from this section of video.

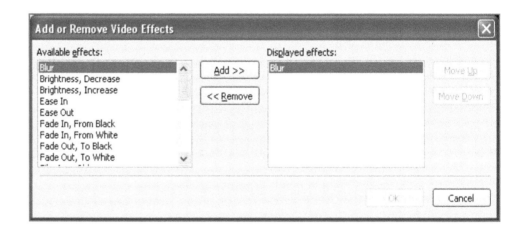

Figure 1.19 Adding or removing video effects

You can add other features, such as opening titles and closing credits, as well as sections of text in between the various sections of video. To do this:

- Select 'Make titles and credits' from the 'Edit' menu options.
- Work through the various sections, adding the text you want to be displayed before, during or after the movie.

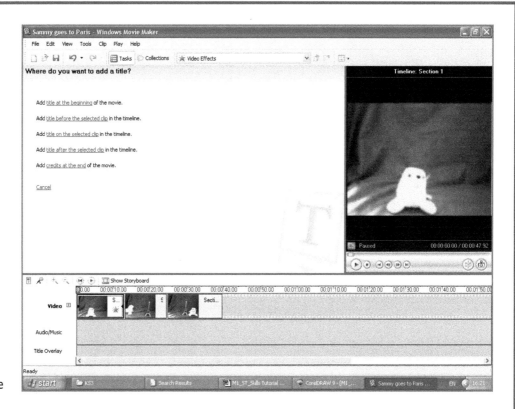

Figure 1.20 Adding a title

You can also add a music file by clicking on the 'Import audio or music' option under 'Capture video'.

Finally, you need to save the movie into a format that means it can be viewed on other computers and devices.

- Select 'Save to my computer'.
- Select a suitable folder and give the movie a name.

It will now be saved as a wmv or windows media video file, which will play with any of the standard media players such as Windows Media Player or Apple Quicktime.

2 Computer games

In this module you will use a range of ICT skills and knowledge to:
> Evaluate a computer game and suggest how it could be improved
> Create a design for a computer game
> Create a computer game
> Test and then make changes to your computer game
> Create a user guide

Introduction

Figure 2.1 Halo

In this module you will be using ICT to play, edit and create your own computer games.

There are many different types of computer games, ranging from basic 2D graphics games that you might play on a mobile phone to full 3D games designed for games consoles. Some computer games are quite simple and perhaps just have one level where the player plays against the computer. Some games are played over several levels, with each level harder than the next, and can take days to complete. These days, many people play computer games online against people from all over the world.

People who write computer games are called 'programmers'. Writing computer games can be quite complicated because you have to think of everything that might happen in the game. Popular console games such as Halo are written by teams of programmers and take many months to design, create and test.

We are going to go through the whole process of designing, writing and then testing a 2D game using a piece of software called Game Maker 7, which is available free from the Internet.

Writing instructions

The basic process of creating a computer game is to write sets of instructions. You have done this before when you looked at computer control in InteraCT 1 and 2. You will be doing the same thing here – writing instructions to control the computer.

Figure 2.2 Noughts and crosses

Let's look at an example. If you wanted to recreate the game 'noughts and crosses' as a computer game, you would need to give the computer some instructions. The first set of instructions would be to tell the computer to draw out the basic grid. You will need to tell it how big to make the grid and how many squares are needed.

You would then need to program in the rules:

1 If Player 1 clicks in this grid, put a cross.
2 If Player 2 clicks in this grid, put a circle.
3 If Player 1 gets three crosses in a row, then show the message: 'Player 1 wins'.
4 If Player 2 gets three circles in a row, then show the message: 'Player 2 wins'.
5 If the grid is full and no one has three in a row, then show the message: 'Play again'.

You can see that this gets quite complicated quite quickly. This is because the programmer has to tell the computer exactly what to do. The programmer also has to think about what happens if someone tries to do something that is not allowed. For example, what if Player 1 tries to put a cross in a grid that already has a circle in it?

To stop this happening there needs to be two new rules:

> If Player 1 clicks on a grid with a circle in it, show the message: 'Please try again'.
> If Player 2 clicks on a grid with a cross in it, show the message: 'Please try again'.

The systems life cycle

When any new computer system is created, including computer games, the programmer will go through a number of steps (or stages). This is called the 'systems life cycle'. The main stages are shown in the diagram below:

Figure 2.3 The systems life cycle

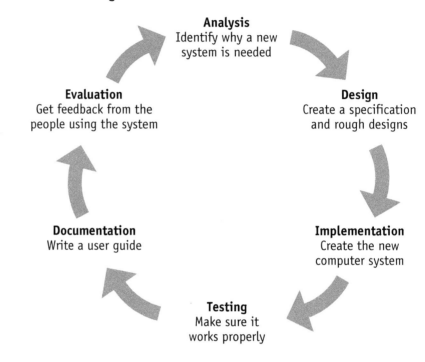

We are going to concentrate on the four main stages: design, implementation, testing and documentation.

Figure 2.4 The digger game

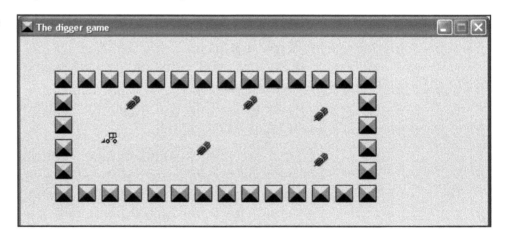

> **Design:** First you must create a clear 'specification'. In this case it will explain what the rules of the game are and what is needed to create it. You should also create rough designs of the game before you start making it.

> **Implementation:** This is where you use games creation software to make your game. We will be using Game Maker 7, which is designed specially for pupils.

 **Skills Tutorial 1**   This tutorial shows you how to get started with Game Maker.

 **Skills Tutorial 2**   This tutorial shows you how to set up your objects so that they do what you want them to during the game.

 Skills Tutorial 3   This tutorial shows you how to create a room.

 **Skills Tutorial 4**   This tutorial shows you how to add a timeline, add a message, and save your game so that it can be played on any computer.

> **Testing:** This is where you check that the game works and does what it is supposed to. You should check the game yourself and get someone else to check it. Companies that write computer games employ games testers. All problems found during testing need to be fixed before the game is released.

> **Documentation:** This is where you write a user guide so that someone who has never used the system before will know how to use it.

 Practical Task: Designing a computer game

Now it's your turn! Open the 'Designing a computer game' worksheet on the website and follow the instructions.

 Practical Task: Creating and testing a computer game

Once you have completed this, you need to fully test the system and get someone else to give it a thorough test too. Open the 'Creating and testing a computer game' worksheet on the website and follow the instructions.

 Written Task: Writing a user guide

Finally, you need to create a user guide so that someone who has never used the game before knows how it works. Open the 'Writing a user guide' worksheet on the website and follow the instructions.

2 | SKILLS TUTORIAL 1

This tutorial will show you how to get started with Game Maker. If you work your way through the whole tutorial it will show you how to create the Digger Game that you have been playing.

Open Game Maker 7. Note that you are using a 'lite' version of the software. This means that it contains fewer options than the full version. However, it does contain enough features to let you make some basic games.

The main window is now displayed and looks like this:

Figure 2.5 Game Maker 7

The software is laid out like most other software you are used to, with a row of menus and toolbars across the top.

The main (grey) window is where you create your games and all of the various components of the game.

On the left-hand side are a number of folders. By clicking on the folders, different windows will open in the main window, allowing you to create and edit different parts of the game.

Before we go any further it is worth explaining the different features that we will be using to create the Digger Game.

● **Sprites:** A sprite is basically an image that is displayed on the screen. For example, the Digger Game contains three sprites: the digger, the blocks used for the walls and the dynamite.

- **Sounds:** These are sound files. You can have various sounds playing when things happen in the game. For example, the Digger Game uses an explosion sound every time the digger hits dynamite.
- **Timelines:** This is where you can set up certain events to happen at certain times. For example, we will use a timeline to set the length of time allowed to complete the game.
- **Objects:** These are things that you use in your game. For example, we will be using the three sprites as objects in our game. This is probably the most difficult thing to understand in Game Maker; as you work through this tutorial you will find out much more about objects.
- **Rooms:** This is the space that you create on the screen for the game to be played in. We only use one room in the Digger Game, but you could create lots of different rooms as part of your own games.

The first stage of creating a game is to create the sprites and objects that you want to use. In simple terms, a sprite is an image. It becomes an object as soon as you use it in the game. For example, the digger is just an image file. In Game Maker we make it into an object, which means that we can do things with it like move it around the screen.

To create a sprite:

- Select 'Resources' from the menu.
- Select 'Create sprite'.

Figure 2.6 Creating a sprite

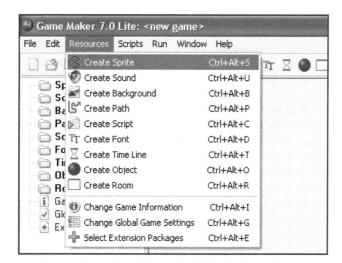

This window will now be displayed:

Figure 2.7 Sprite properties

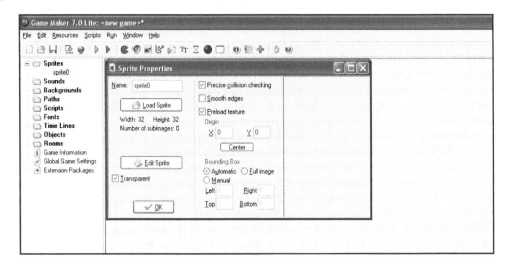

- Under 'Name', type **Digger**.
- Click 'Load Sprite'.

You can now locate the image file that you would like to use. You can use your own image files for this, or Game Maker has some in already.

- Select 'Shovel'.
- Click 'Open'.
- Click on the 'OK' button.

You now repeat this process to create a sprite for the walls and the dynamite.

You now need to create an object, which you do using these sprites.

- Click on 'Resources'.
- Select 'Create object'.

The following window is then displayed:

Figure 2.8 **Figure 2.8** Creating an object

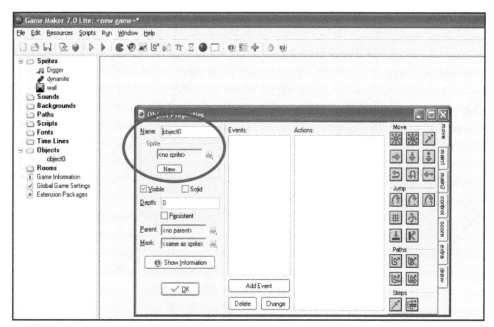

- Under 'Name', type Digger.
- Next to 'Sprite' click on the small icon that looks a little like a drop-down list.
- Select 'Digger' and click 'OK'.
- Repeat this process for the dynamite and the wall, making sure that you choose the appropriate sprite in each case.
- When you do this for the wall, click on the tick box for 'Solid' just below the drop-down list.

This makes the wall a solid object, which means that the digger will not be able to move through it. Instead we can tell it to bounce off.

We also need to add some sounds to use later on. We want two sounds: the first is the sound of an explosion, which we will use when the digger hits a stick of dynamite, the second will be a beep to indicate that the time has run out. The process of creating sounds is very similar to creating sprites:

- Select 'Resources'.
- Click on 'Create sound'.
- Give the sound a name, for example 'explosion'.
- Click on 'Load sound' and choose a suitable sound file.
- Repeat the process for the beep sound that you will use at the end; call this 'gameover'.

You can use your own sound files, or Game Maker has some already.

That is the basic set up. You should save your game as you go along in the usual way. Note that the files have a 'gmk' suffix.

2| SKILLS TUTORIAL 2

This tutorial will show you how to set up your objects so that they do what we want them to during the game. For example, we need to tell the digger to move around when we press the arrow keys. It does **not** do this automatically. We have to program the digger object to do it.

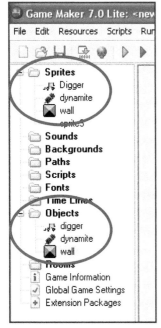

Figure 2.9 New sprites and objects

Figure 2.10 Object properties

On the left-hand panel, you will now see the new sprites and objects that you have created.

If you ever need to change the sprites or objects you can get back to them by double-clicking on them from here.

It is unlikely that you will want to change your sprites once you have created them, but you will need to work on the objects.

We'll start with the digger.

● Under 'Objects', double-click on 'digger'.

The objects options window is now displayed:

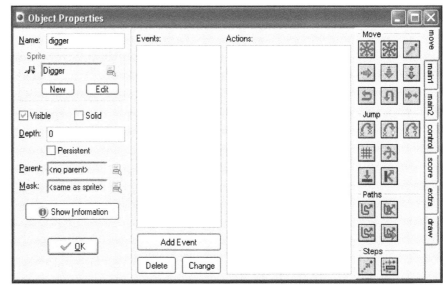

Game Maker uses 'events' to make things happen. An event might be something like the player pressing a key on the keyboard or using the mouse. We have to tell the object what it is supposed to do after an event.

For example, if the player presses the left arrow key, we need to program the game so that the digger object moves left.

● Click on 'Add event'.

The list of possible events is now shown:

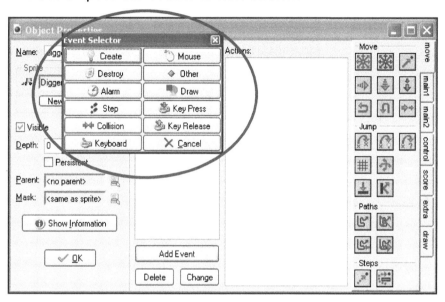

Figure 2.11 Event selector

● Click on 'Keyboard'.
● Select <left> from the list.

You will see that it has put this in the 'Events' box.

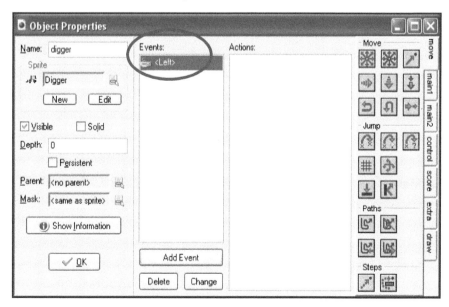

Figure 2.12 Selecting the left arrow key

You now need to tell it what it should do if the left arrow key is pressed:

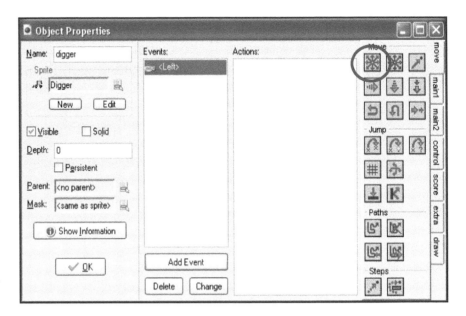

Figure 2.13 Programming the left arrow key

- Click and hold on the icon that shows nine red arrows.
- Drag it into the 'Actions' window and release it.

When you release it will read 'Start moving in a direction' in the 'Actions' box, and this window will be displayed:

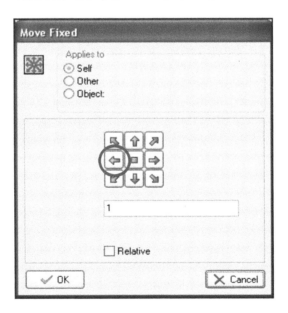

Figure 2.14 Setting the direction and speed

- Click on the left arrow and it will turn red.
- Set the speed to 1.
- Click 'OK'.

You have now told the computer that when someone presses the left arrow key, the digger object should move left.

You need to work through this process three more times for the right, up and down arrow keys. Make sure you click on the appropriate arrow in the screen above and set the speed to 1 in each case.

When you have finished the object window should look something like this:

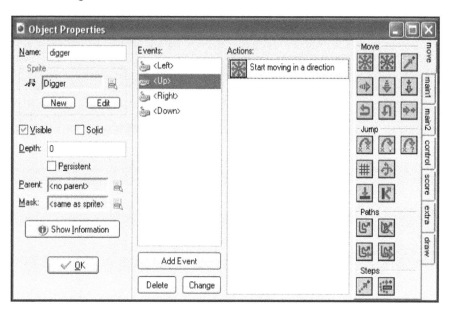

Figure 2.15 All arrow keys are set

We now need to tell the digger object what to do if it hits the wall or if it hits the dynamite. This time the 'event' is going to be a collision between the digger and the wall or dynamite. We'll do the wall first:

- Click 'Add Event'.
- Select 'Collision'.
- Select 'Wall'.
- From the icons on the left select 'Bounce against solid objects' and drag it into the 'Actions' window.

You can hold the mouse over each icon and it will tell you what it is. In this case we want this one:

Figure 2.16 Bounce against solid objects icon

- Another window is displayed on which you can just click 'OK'.

This instruction means that when the digger hits the wall it will bounce off and carry on moving.

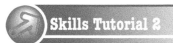

The settings for the dynamite are slightly different as we need the dynamite to make a noise and disappear.

- Click 'Add Event'.
- Select 'Collision'.
- Select 'Dynamite'.

We want three things to happen:

- The explosion sound is triggered.
- The score goes up by 1.
- The digger bounces off and carries on moving.

To trigger the explosion:

- Select 'Main 1' from the tabs on the right-hand side, as shown below:

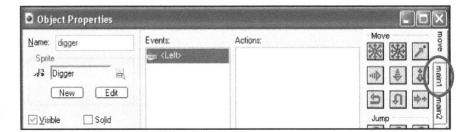

Figure 2.17 Selecting the 'Main 1' tab

- Now drag the sound icon into the 'Actions' box.

Figure 2.18 Sound icon

- A new window is displayed, as shown:

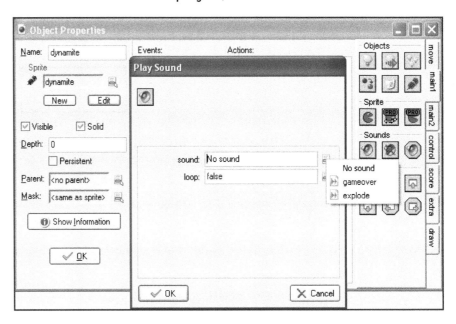

Figure 2.19 Selecting the sound

- Click on the drop-down list next to 'No sound' and change this to 'explosion'.
- Now click on the 'Move' tab and drag the 'Bounce against solid objects' icon into the 'Actions' box as you have done before.
- Now select the 'Score' tab on the right-hand side and drag on the 'Set score' icon (which is the first one). Remember that you can hold the mouse over the icon to see what it does.

This screen is then displayed:

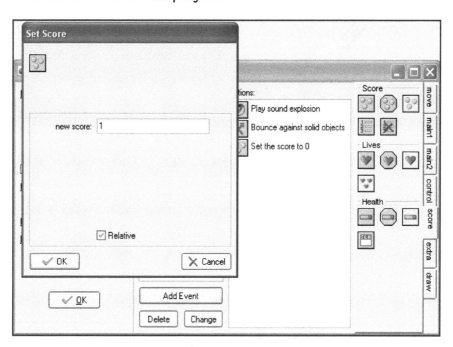

Figure 2.20 Setting the score

- Set the 'new score' to 1 and click on the 'Relative' box.

There is one more object to set. We need to make the dynamite disappear when it is hit by the digger. To do this:

- Double-click on the dynamite object on the left-hand side.
- Click 'Add event'.
- Select 'Collision'.
- Select 'Digger'.
- Drag the 'Jump to a given position' icon into the 'Actions' window. It is under the 'Main' tab and looks like this:

Figure 2.21 Jump to a given position icon

- Click 'OK' on the next window.

This moves the dynamite out of the game play area and puts it in the top left-hand corner of the screen to show that it has been hit.

2 SKILLS TUTORIAL 3

In this tutorial you will learn how to create a room.

- Select 'Resources' and 'Create room'.

This window is now displayed. This represents the game playing area.

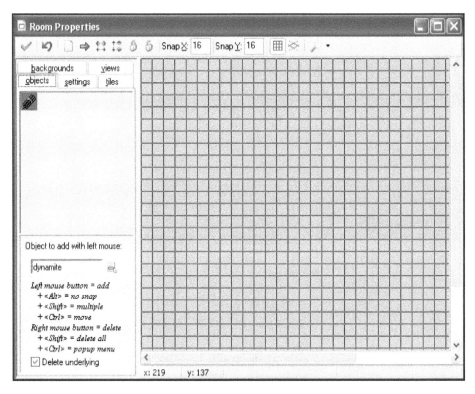

Figure 2.22 Room properties

You can now add any of the objects into the room. We need to do three main things:

- Build a wall out of the wall blocks.
- Add five sticks of dynamite.
- Add one digger.

Figure 2.23 Wall, dynamite and digger icons

To create the wall:

- Click on the dynamite picture under Objects and select the wall picture.
- Now move into the main room and click wherever you want to put a building block.
- To delete a block, right-click on it.
- Continue until you have built a complete room.

The room can be any shape and size you like. You must make sure that there are no gaps where the digger could escape. Remember that the digger will bounce off the wall when it hits it.

To add the dynamite:

- Click on the wall picture under Objects and select the dynamite picture.
- Click to add the dynamite object to the room. Right-click to delete.

In the original game we put five sticks of dynamite in the room, but you could have more or fewer to make the game easier or harder.

- Follow the same process to add the digger.

You only need one digger – you need to put it wherever you want the starting position to be at the beginning of the game.

2 SKILLS TUTORIAL 4

In this tutorial you will learn how to add a timeline and a message, and how to save your game so that it can be played on any computer.

We need to add a timeline so that the game ends after a set amount of time. When the time runs out a message needs to be displayed offering the player another game.

To add a timeline:

- Select 'Resources' and 'Create timeline'.
- Give it a name, for example 'Timer'.
- Click on 'Add'.

The following window is displayed:

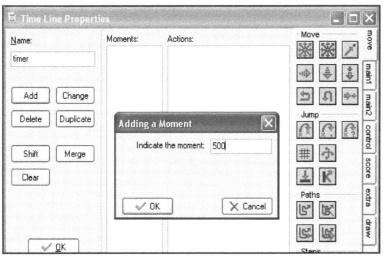

Figure 2.24 Adding a timeline

You have to tell it what the 'Moment' is. By this it means how long you want the timer to run before it is triggered. In this case, we want it to run for about 20 seconds and then end the game showing a message.

You have to type in the number in 'steps', not in seconds. There are 30 steps per second, so 600 steps would be exactly 20 seconds. In this case it is set to 500 steps, which is about 16 seconds.

You now need to drag three different icons into the Actions box. This process is exactly the same as you have used throughout the tutorial. You need to find the appropriate icon and drag it into the Actions box:

- Drag in a 'Play sound' icon from the 'Main1' tab and set it to play the 'gameover' sound that you created earlier.
- Drag in a 'Display a message' icon from the 'Main2' tab and type your message into the box provided. This is the message that is displayed at the end of the game.

- Drag in a 'Restart the game' icon from the 'Main2' tab.
- Click 'OK'.

You now need to attach this timer to one of the objects in the game:

- Double-click on the dynamite object on the left-hand side under the 'Objects' folder.
- Click on 'Main2' and drag a 'Set Time line' icon into the 'Actions' box.
- Click on the drop-down list next to the 'Time Line' box and select 'Timer'.
- Click 'OK'.

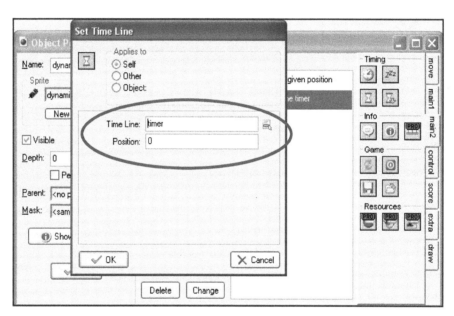

Figure 2.25 Attaching a timer

You are now ready to play the game!

You can play at any time by clicking on the 'Run the game' icon in the toolbar at the top of the screen. You have probably done this already as you have been making and testing your game.

The final thing to do is to save the game as an executable (exe) file. You have already been saving it as a gmk file, but this will only work on a computer that has Game Maker installed on it.

To save it in a format that will run on any computer:

- Select 'File' from the main menu.
- Select 'Create executable'.
- Give your game a name and save it in a suitable folder.

You can now give people the file and they can load it and play it on their computers.

3 Shape recognition

Learning Objectives	In this module you will use a range of ICT skills and knowledge to:

> **Use a programming language to create shapes**
> **Write precise and efficient programming instructions**
> **Use a spreadsheet model designed to help young children recognise shapes**
> **Make changes to an existing model or create your own**

Introduction

In this module you will be using ICT to create shapes using a programming language. You will also be using a spreadsheet model to adapt or make an educational game that helps young children to recognise shapes.

Programming languages are used to create computer software. There are hundreds of different programming languages available. In Module 2 you used a programming language called Game Maker, which is designed specifically for making games.

In this module you will be using Logo, which is mainly used for creating shapes. There are more than a hundred versions of Logo available, some of which do much more complex things. We will be using MSWLogo, which is free. In your school you may have a different version.

Programming basics

Most programming languages work by typing in instructions that tell the computer what to do. These instructions are called 'programming code'. In this module you will be acting as the computer programmer, writing instructions for the computer to follow.

This is very similar to the work you have done on computer control. With computer control you input instructions using a flowchart; in this case you will type instructions straight into the computer.

Here's an example of some computer code that tells the computer to draw a square.

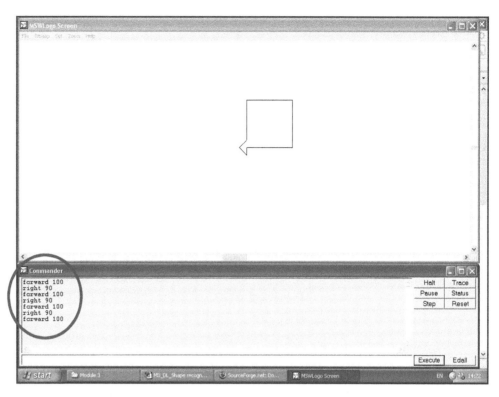

Figure 3.1 Programming code

Notice that there is a triangle in the centre of the main screen (called a turtle). This shows where the drawing will start from and the direction. Here are some of the instructions:

forward 100   this moves the turtle forward 100 units, drawing a line

right 90   this turns the turtle 90 degrees to the right

left 90   this turns the turtle 90 degrees to the left

Skills Tutorial 1   This tutorial shows you how to get started in MSWLogo.

Debugging

Computers are basically stupid as they only do what they are told. Therefore if you get the code wrong, the computer will do the wrong thing. If this happens you will see it has gone wrong and you then need to 'debug' your code. This means you have to find the error and put it right.

Look at the following example, which is supposed to draw a square:

forward 100
left 90
forward 100
forward 100
left 90
forward 100
left 90
forward 100

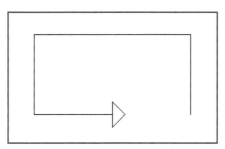

You might be able to spot the error just by looking at the code. It is easy to see that something has gone wrong as the shape it has drawn is not a square. You would need to work out where the code has gone wrong and edit it.

Efficiency

As well as getting the code correct, you should also try and make it as efficient as possible. This means that you use as few lines of code as possible. If you look at the correct code to create a square, you can see that the same two lines of code are repeated four times:

forward 100
right 90

This can be written as one line of code, which is much more efficient:

repeat 4 [forward 100 right 90]

You could be even more efficient than that. For example, if you wanted to use the square again you could save these instructions and call them 'Square'. This means that every time you type the word Square, a square will be displayed on the screen.

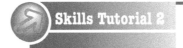 **Skills Tutorial 2** This tutorial shows you how to use the REPEAT command and how to save your commands so that you can use them again later.

Skills Tutorial 3 This tutorial shows you how to create a square of any size using a variable.

☞ **Practical Task:** Creating shapes in Logo
It's your turn to create some shapes using Logo. Open the 'Creating shapes in Logo' worksheet on the website and follow the instructions.

Modelling

Finally in this module, we are going to use a spreadsheet model that has been set up like a game for young children to play. This model uses some basic 2D and 3D shapes and asks children to match the shapes to the correct descriptions.

The spreadsheet model checks whether the child has got the answer correct and then gives them a score out of six.

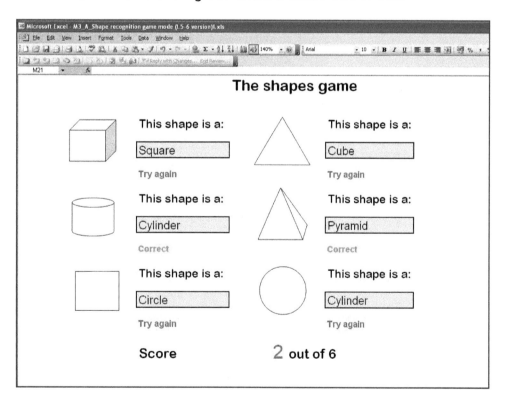

Figure 3.2 The shapes game

☞ **Practical Task:** The shape recognition model
In this task you will make changes to the model or even make your own version of it. Open 'The shape recognition game model' on the website and follow the instructions.

3| SKILLS TUTORIAL 1

This tutorial will show you how to get started in MSWLogo.

Open MSWLogo and you will see this screen:

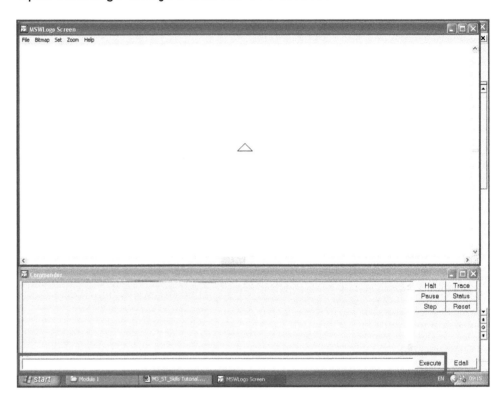

Figure 3.3 MSWLogo

The top half of the screen is where you will see the shapes that you create. Notice that there is a triangle (called a turtle) in the centre of the screen. You control this turtle by typing in commands.

In the bottom half of the screen is the 'Commander', which shows you all of the commands you have typed in.

The white bar at the bottom of the screen (highlighted) is where you type in the commands.

- Click in the white bar and type: forward 100.
- Press ENTER or click on the 'Execute' button.

You will see that this moves the turtle 100 units, drawing a straight line as it moves. Notice that the command now appears in the Commander window to remind you of what commands you have typed in.

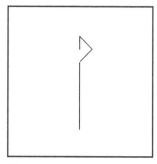

Figure 3.4 Single line

Notice too that the direction that the turtle (arrow) is pointing shows you which direction it is moving.

- Type in: right 90.
- Press ENTER or click on the 'Execute' button.

You will see that this turns the turtle through a 90 degree angle.

- Type in: forward 100.
- Press ENTER or click on the 'Execute' button.

Another line is drawn.

You can now continue using these two commands until you have a square on the screen.

There are a couple of shortcuts you can use however:

- You can type FD instead of forward and RT instead of right.
- You can type all of the instructions on one line rather than pressing ENTER after every line.

To start with it is best to type each new command on a new line. This way, if you go wrong, it is easier to work out where.

There are lots of other commands that Logo uses: some of the main ones are listed below with an explanation of what they do. Note that it does not matter whether you use capitals or lower-case letters.

Command	What it does
Forward or FD	Moves the turtle forward. You have to tell it how far to move, e.g. 100.
Back or BK	Moves the turtle backwards. You have to tell it how far to move, e.g. 100.
Right or RT	Rotates the turtle to the right. You have to tell it what angle to turn, e.g. 90.
Left or LT	Rotates the turtle to the left. You have to tell it what angle to turn, e.g. 90.
Penup or PU	Lifts the pen off the paper, which means that you can move the turtle without it drawing a line. This is useful if you are drawing more complicated shapes and need to move the turtle to different positions.
Pendown or PD	Puts the pen on the paper, which means that when you move the turtle it will draw a line.
Clearscreen or CS	Clears the screen completely and resets the turtle in the centre.
Cleartext or CT	Clears the contents of the Commander window. This is useful when you are experimenting as it can get full of commands.
Circle	Draws a circle. You have to tell it how big you want it to be, e.g. 100.
Repeat	Repeats the same command. You have to tell it how many times to repeat the instruction.

At this stage you might want to spend some time experimenting with the basic commands and drawing some shapes. For example, you could try writing your initials.

3 | SKILLS TUTORIAL 2

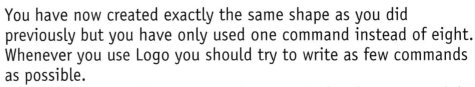

This tutorial will show you how to use the REPEAT command and how to save your commands so that you can use them again later.

In the previous session you created a square by typing in the following commands:

> **Forward 100**
> **Right 90**
> **Forward 100**
> **Right 90**
> **Forward 100**
> **Right 90**
> **Forward 100**
> **Right 90**

You may have noticed that you were typing in the same two lines over and over again – four times to be precise.

Wherever you find yourself repeating the same commands, you can use the REPEAT command to make it easier and more efficient.

● Type in **CS** and press ENTER. This clears the shape and resets the turtle.
● Type in **CT** and press ENTER. This clears the Commander window.

These two commands are useful as they basically get you back to where you started.

● Type in: **repeat 4 [fd 100 rt 90]**.

You have now created exactly the same shape as you did previously but you have only used one command instead of eight. Whenever you use Logo you should try to write as few commands as possible.

The chances are that once you have created a shape, you might want to use it over and over again. Instead of typing the command in several times, you can save your commands into a 'procedure'. For example, we can create a procedure called 'Square'

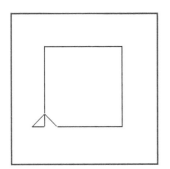

Figure 3.5 Square

that contains the commands for drawing a square. Every time we want a square from then on, we can just type in SQUARE without having to type in all the commands.

To do this:

● Type in **CS CT** and press ENTER.

This will clear the screen and the Commander window.

● Type in **Edit "Square** and press ENTER.

This will open a new window called the editor, which looks like this.

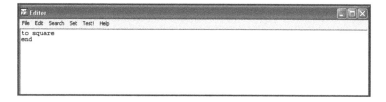

Figure 3.6 Editor window

This editor works just like any other text editor – you just need to type into it. Notice that there is already some text in the editor that reads: 'to square' and 'end'.

You have to leave 'to square' as the first line and 'end' as the last line, and type your instructions in between the two.

● We want to create a square, so you need to type: repeat 4 [fd 100 rt 90]

It should look like this:

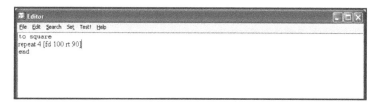

Figure 3.7 Creating the procedure

● Click on 'File'.
● Select 'Save and Exit'.

You have created the procedure; to draw a square now all you need to do is:

● Type in **square**.

The square will now be displayed. Every time you type 'square' a new square is created at the position of the turtle.

3 | SKILLS TUTORIAL 3

This tutorial will show you how to create a square of any size using a 'variable'.

There are likely to be times when we want to use one of our procedures, for example the square like the one we have just made, but where you want different sizes. Our procedure only draws squares that are 100 by 100 units.

We could create lots of different procedures for different-sized squares, or we could use a variable. The idea of this is that we know we want a square but the size we want is variable. Therefore, instead of telling it to make a square that's 100 by 100 units, we can set it to whatever size we want.

- Type in **CS CT** and press ENTER.
- Type in **edit "square**
- In the editor you need three lines, as follows:

> **to square :length**
> **repeat 4 [fd :length rt 90]**
> **end**

Figure 3.8 Replacing the fixed length

```
Editor
File   Edit   Search   Set   Test!   Help
to square :length
repeat 4 [fd :length rt 90]
end
```

- Click on 'File' and 'Save and Exit'.

What you have done here is replace the fixed length of 100 with a variable length.

To create your square:

- Type in **square 100** and press ENTER.

This will create a square 100 by 100 units.

- Type in **square 200** and press ENTER.

This will create a square 200 by 200 units.

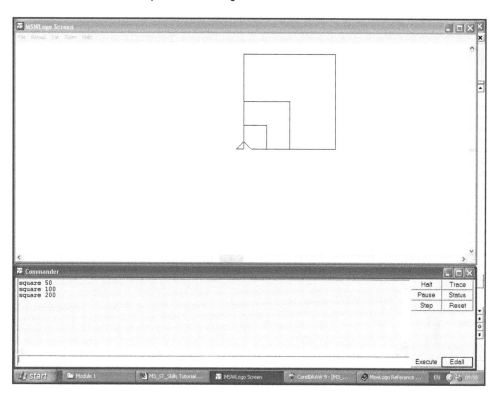

Figure 3.9 Creating squares of different sizes

Using this method you can create a square of any size very quickly and efficiently without having to type in lots of commands.

4 Creating a social networking website

| Learning Objectives | In this module you will use a range of ICT skills and knowledge to: |

> **Plan the layout and content of web pages**
> **Decide what software to use to create web pages**
> **Create web pages**
> **Create a suitable structure for a series of web pages**
> **Consider aspects of safety and security**

Introduction

In this module you will be using ICT to plan, design and then create a social networking web page. Social networking websites are where you can set up a page that includes information about yourself (a profile), pictures, videos, links to other websites, a comments area, blogs, quizzes, polls and just about anything else you can think of.

You can also view your friends' profiles and create links between your page and your online friends. Other people who come across your page might post comments or ask if they can be linked to your page as one of your friends.

If you haven't been on a social networking site, you will need to take a look at one before you do anything else. The three most well-known ones are MySpace, Bebo and Facebook. The idea behind all of them is the same. Let's take a look at a MySpace page to see how they work.

A typical social networking web page

Most social networking sites have lots of different features to them – that's what makes them so interesting. We can see some of the main features at the top of the next page.

When you link to a friend, in turn you get access to all of the links from their page and you can see the profiles of other people on the network. A large network of online friends can build up very quickly.

Main details
showing a
photograph,
name, age
and where
the person
lives. Notice
the links to
other pictures
and videos.

Links to a
blog, which is
a bit like an
online diary.

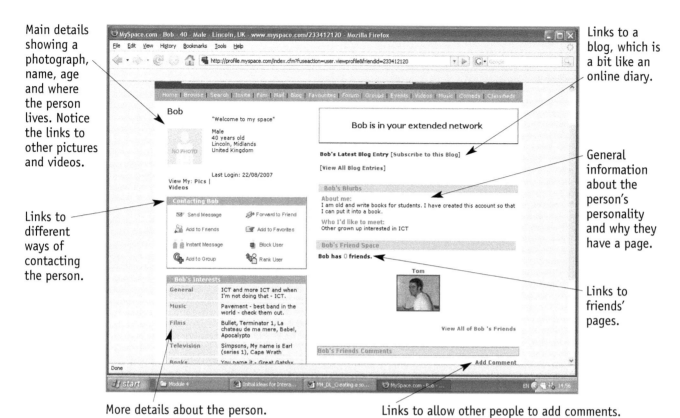

General
information
about the
person's
personality
and why they
have a page.

Links to
different
ways of
contacting
the person.

Links to
friends'
pages.

More details about the person.

Links to allow other people to add comments.

Figure 4.1 MySpace

Planning your pages

In this module we will work through a detailed plan of what we want on our web pages. We will use MySpace, Bebo or Facebook as an example of what we are trying to create, but we will then go on to plan and create pages of our own.

To start with you need to plan what you want to put on your pages and then think about what ICT tools you can use to create the web pages.

 Practical Task: Planning your web pages

Open the 'Planning your web pages' document on the website and follow the instructions.

You need to think carefully about:

> What information you want to include.
> What pictures and videos to use – you may even create some just for this web page.
> How many pages you will need.
> How the pages link together.
> What external links to include.
> What overall design you want for the page.

Figure 4.2 Facebook

Creating your page

It's now time to create the page using whatever web-design software you think is most suitable.

 Practical Task: Creating your web pages

Open the 'Creating your web pages' document on the website and follow the instructions.

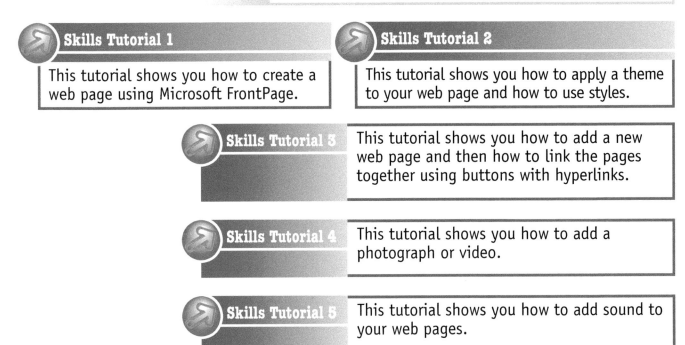

Skills Tutorial 1

This tutorial shows you how to create a web page using Microsoft FrontPage.

Skills Tutorial 2

This tutorial shows you how to apply a theme to your web page and how to use styles.

Skills Tutorial 3

This tutorial shows you how to add a new web page and then how to link the pages together using buttons with hyperlinks.

Skills Tutorial 4

This tutorial shows you how to add a photograph or video.

Skills Tutorial 5

This tutorial shows you how to add sound to your web pages.

Thinking about personal safety

There is a lot of concern at the moment about how safe you are when you are on the Internet.

Pupils reminded of internet safety

Internet savvy schoolchildren are to be reminded about the dangers of revealing personal details online as part of an expanding web safety campaign.

The Child Exploitation and Online Protection Centre (CEOP) launched a national campaign, including talks, workshops and a film featuring a boy who was abused by a paedophile whom he met in an online chatroom.

Over 1,000 police officers, teachers and child protection teams will deliver the programme to schools across the UK examining issues like social networking, gaming sites and chat rooms.

CEOP believe that a million children will have taken part in the sessions by March 2007, with other phases to be rolled out on an ongoing basis.

Jim Gamble, the head of CEOP, said he hoped the warnings set out in the ThinkuKnow programme would help children rethink whether they would physically meet up with people they befriended online.

"The internet is not infested with paedophiles, but one paedophile on the internet can pretend to be many different people."

"We've accepted we can't tackle the problem ourselves."

"Children are the most technology savvy people, so we want to empower children to protect themselves and their peers."

"And this will mean the next generation of parents will also be more informed."

A facility has also been introduced on the ThinkuKnow website which allows children to report any incidents where there has been inappropriate online contact.

Figure 4.3 From BBC Online

In this final task you will be asked to think about the dangers and ways in which you can keep yourself safe.

 Written Task: Internet safety
Open the 'Internet Safety' worksheet on the website and follow the instructions.

SKILLS TUTORIAL 1

This tutorial will show you how to create a web page using Microsoft FrontPage. We will use a horse web page as an example.

- Open Microsoft FrontPage.

You will see a blank page with three tabs in the bottom left-hand corner. You use the Normal view to design your web page. You can also see the HTML view, which is the code that is created for you. You can also click for a preview to see how it will look when viewed in a browser.

- Type the title: **Welcome to my horse page.**
- Highlight it and set the font to Arial size 7.

Notice that web design software uses a different system for font sizes. Size 7 is actually font size 36.
   To add the line:

- Position the cursor on the line beneath the title.
- Select 'Insert'.
- Select 'Horizontal line'.

Figure 4.4 Adding a line

This will add a line across the width of the web page.

- Now type the two lines:

> **My hobby is horse riding.**
> **Here is a picture of my horse Barnie.**

- Highlight the text and set it to Times point size 4.
- Highlight the word 'Barnie' and set this to bold.
- Press 'Enter' again.

To insert a picture:

- Select 'Insert'.
- Select 'Picture'.
- Select 'From file'.
- Find the HORSE.BMP file.

You may need to re-size the image by dragging from the corners. To re-position the picture:

- Click on the 'Position absolutely' icon on the Picture toolbar in the bottom left-hand corner as shown:

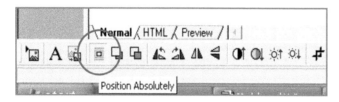

Figure 4.5 Re-positioning the picture

- You can now move the picture anywhere on the page.

To set the background to green:

- Select 'Format'.
- Select 'Background'.

This screen is displayed:

- Select the 'Background' tab.
- Select 'green' where shown and press 'OK'.

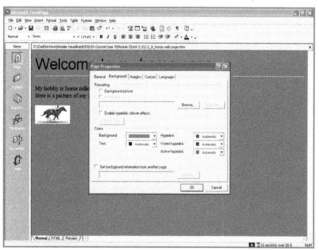

Figure 4.6 Setting the background colour

To preview the website:

- Click the 'Preview' tab in the bottom left-hand corner.

To save:

- Select 'File' and 'Save'.

SKILLS TUTORIAL 2

This tutorial will show you how to apply a theme to your web page and how to use styles.

- Open a new page in Microsoft FrontPage.
- Select 'Format'.
- Select 'Theme'.

The following screen is displayed, which gives you a range of themes to choose from. The themes include a background colour and patterns, and fonts styles and sizes for various styles. For example, it shows you what the Heading styles look like and what the Bullet styles look like.

- Select 'Arcs'.

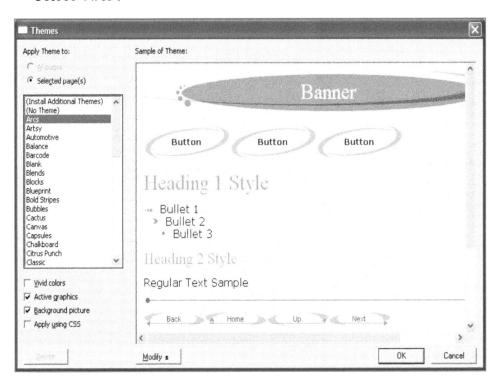

Figure 4.7 Themes

- Click 'OK'.

The only thing you will see at the moment is the background pattern, as there is nothing else on the page yet.

- On the top line, type in: **Welcome to my web page.**
- Highlight the text and then click on the Styles drop-down box, as shown:

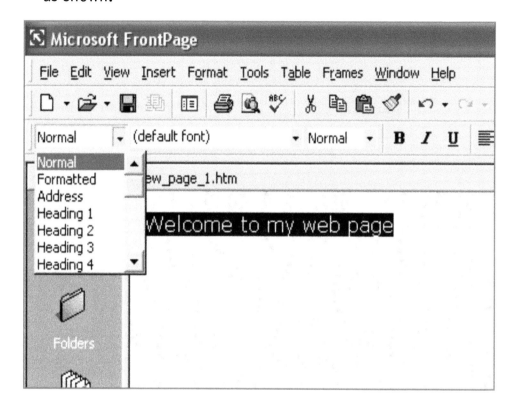

Figure 4.8 Setting the styles for Heading 1

- Select 'Heading 1'.

You will see that the font style, size and colour have been changed on your text.

Once you have selected a theme and a style, it means that whenever you use Heading 1, it will always be in exactly the same font size, style and colour. You can use any of the other styles in exactly the same way. This way you know you are being consistent.

Save this web page as 'Web page for skills tutorial'.

SKILLS TUTORIAL 3

This tutorial will show you how to add a new page and then how to link the pages together using buttons with hyperlinks.

- Open the 'Web page for skills tutorial' page if it is not already open.
- Click on the small arrow next to the New page icon as shown:

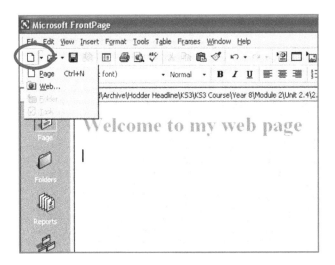

Figure 4.9 Adding a new page

- Select 'Page' and a new blank page will be displayed.

You can now work on this page in the normal way. The first thing you should do is set the theme to the same theme used on the first page, and use the same styles for the text, for example Heading 1 for the main title.

To switch between this page and the original page:

- Select 'Window' from the menu and all the pages that are open will be displayed there. If you have saved the page then the folder and file name will be shown. If you have not saved the page it will be listed as **new page.htm***.

To add a button with a hyperlink:

- Make sure that the first page is open.
- Select 'Insert'.
- Select 'Component'.
- Select 'Hover button'.

This creates a button with text on it, which can be used as a hyperlink.

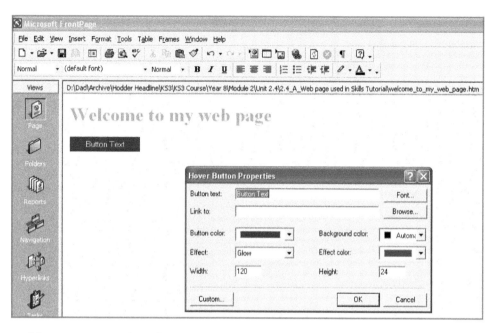

Figure 4.10 Adding a
button with a hyperlink

● You can type in what text you want to appear on the button
where it says 'Button text'.

To create a link to a specific page:

● Click on the 'Browse' button.

A list of pages will now be shown and you can click on the page
that you want to link to. You can link to any other page here:

● Click on the second page.

If you want to link to an external page, that is, one on the Internet,
you can type in the full Internet address where it says 'URL'.
   You can also change the options for how the button will be
displayed:

● Click on 'OK'.

To test the link works:

● Click on the 'Preview' tab in the bottom left-hand corner.

When you put the mouse over the button it will change colour.
When you click on it, it will open Page 2.

● You now need to add another button on Page 2 to take you
back to Page 1.

Every time you add a new page to a website, you have to think
about how you will link to and from the new page to the existing
pages.
   You can now click back on the 'Normal' tab so that you can
carry on designing your web page.

4 SKILLS TUTORIAL 4

This tutorial will show you how to add a photograph or video.

- Open Page 2 of your 'Web page for skills tutorial' file as an example to work with.
- Click on the page where you would like the photograph or video to be displayed (you can always move it later).
- Click on 'Insert'.
- Click on 'Picture'.

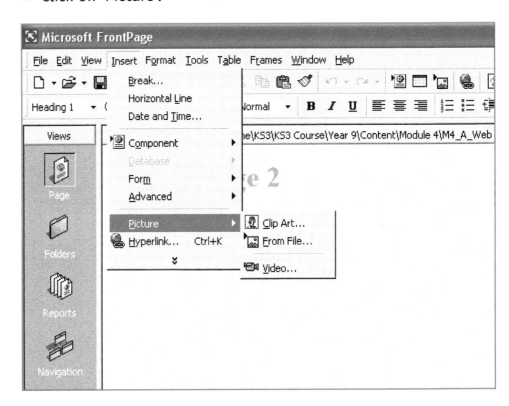

Figure 4.11 Adding a picture

You can select to insert an image from a file and then browse for the photograph that you want to add. This will normally be a JPEG file. You will need to know which folder it is stored in on your computer.

When you have found the photograph you want:

● Double-click on it to add it to the page.

To add a video:

● Click on 'Insert', 'Picture' and then select 'Video'.

You then need to browse through your folders to find the video:

● Double-click on it to add it to your page.

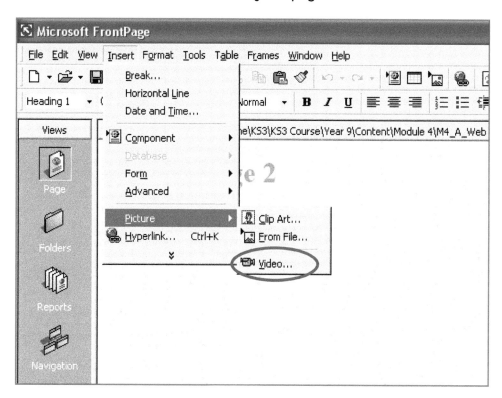

Figure 4.12 Adding a video

4 | SKILLS TUTORIAL 5

This tutorial will show you how to add sound to your web pages.

To add sounds that play when the page is loaded:

● Right click anywhere on the page.
● Select 'Page properties'.

The following screen is displayed:

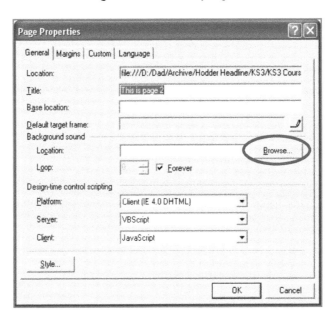

Figure 4.13 Page properties

● Select 'Browse'.

You now need to browse through the folders to find the sound file that you would like to use. This will play all the time when the page is loaded. To prevent this:

● Uncheck the 'Forever' box and select how many times you want the sound to play.

You can also add sounds that will play when you hold the mouse pointer over a hover button. To do this:

● Add a hover button.
● Right-click on the hover button and select 'Properties'.

You will now see this screen:

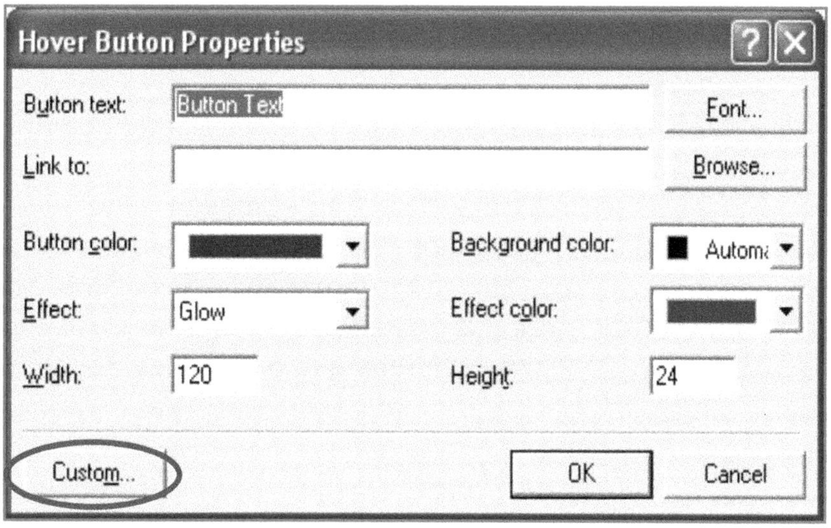

Figure 4.14 Hover button properties

- Select 'Custom'.

You will then see this screen:

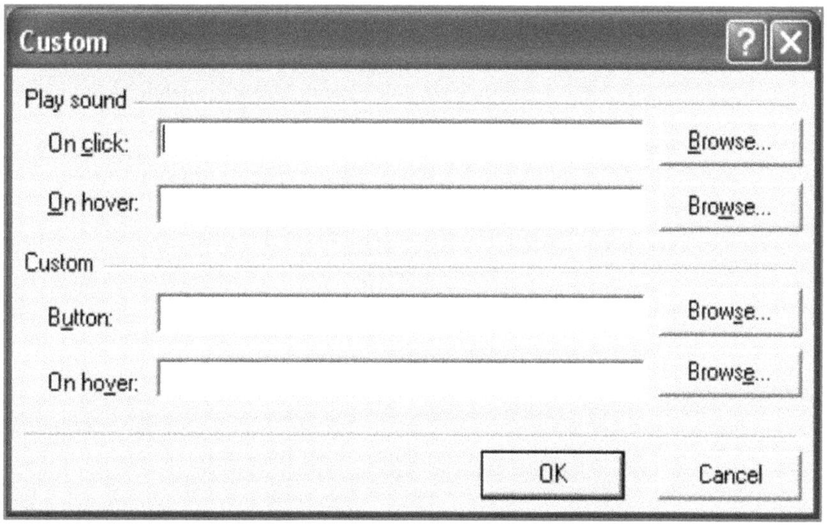

Figure 4.15 Customising how the sound is played

You can now select whether you want the sound to play when you click on the button ('On click') or when you hover over the button with the mouse pointer ('On hover').

You will need to browse your folders to find the sound files that you want to play.

There are many other options in Microsoft FrontPage, including adding marquees (which is text that scrolls across the page), text boxes and Banner Ads (which are adverts that you see on many web pages). You should experiment with these options and add them to your web pages if your think they are suitable.

5 Crime solving

In this module you will use a range of ICT skills and knowledge to:

> Search and sort a database
> Interrogate data to find the solution to a problem
> Use and adapt a spreadsheet model to simulate real-life events
> Create a presentation for a specific audience
> Make decisions and provide evidence to back them up

Introduction

In this module you will be using ICT to solve a crime. You will watch an animation where you will be given some facts and eyewitness accounts about a crime. You will then use this information and other data to work out who you think has committed the crime.

Just like real-life you will be under pressure to get a result. The victim and the press are keen to know how you are getting on and you will have to keep them updated with your progress.

As you work through you will recreate the events to find out who might have committed the crime. Finally you must make an arrest and then find out whether you have arrested the right person.

Figure 5.1 Inspector Baxter at the crime scene

Getting a list of suspects

You will be helping Inspector Baxter. The first thing you need to do is to watch 'The Diamond Robbery (Part 1)' to find out about the crime.

Here's what Inspector Baxter wrote down:

Figure 5.2 Pages from Inspector Baxter's notebook

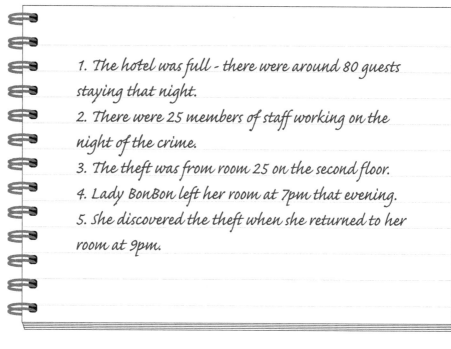

1. The hotel was full – there were around 80 guests staying that night.
2. There were 25 members of staff working on the night of the crime.
3. The theft was from room 25 on the second floor.
4. Lady BonBon left her room at 7pm that evening.
5. She discovered the theft when she returned to her room at 9pm.

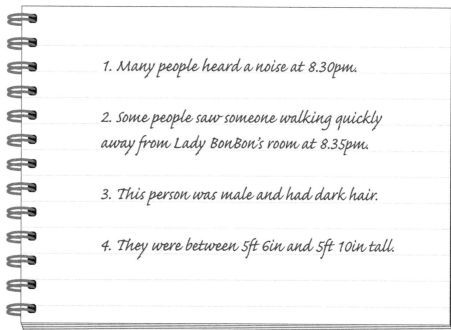

1. Many people heard a noise at 8.30pm.

2. Some people saw someone walking quickly away from Lady BonBon's room at 8.35pm.

3. This person was male and had dark hair.

4. They were between 5ft 6in and 5ft 10in tall.

It's now time for your first task. You have been given two databases. One contains a list of all the guests who were staying that night. The other is a list of every member of staff. You need to come up with a list of suspects for the crime.

 Practical Task: Suspects

Open the 'Suspects' worksheet on the website and follow the instructions.

The reconstruction

You have now narrowed down your list of suspects. In your list are people who were in the hotel at the time and fit the description given by the eyewitnesses. You need to narrow down your list. Some of the suspects were seen in different parts of the hotel at around the time the crime took place.

Inspector Baxter needs to check this out. For example, if Eric Pringle was seen on the 4th floor at 8.40pm, would it be possible for him to have committed the crime on the 2nd floor at 8.35pm and then get back to the 4th floor by 8.40pm?

He decides that he needs to do a reconstruction – he needs to recreate the crime to find out where everyone was and whether they could have done it.

It's time to find out once and for all who the criminal is.

 Practical Task:

Reconstruction

Open the 'Reconstruction' worksheet on the website and follow the instructions.

 **Figure 5.3** Inspector Baxter and Lady BonBon in the hotel lobby

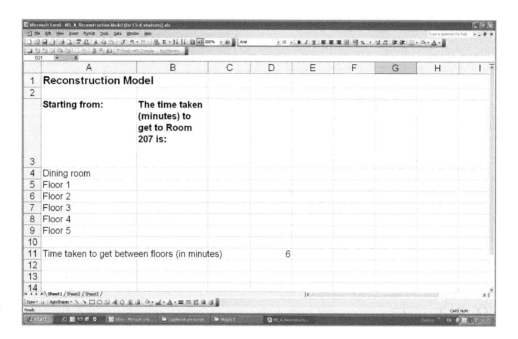

Figure 5.4 Reconstruction model

The press conference

Inspector Baxter is under pressure to get results. You are not quite ready to identify the suspect yet, but you can explain what you have found out up to now.

You are going to prepare a statement and a presentation to give at a press conference.

> **Practical Task:** Press conference
>
> **Open the 'Press conference' worksheet on the website and follow the instructions.**

Coming to a conclusion

You should now have a fairly clear idea of who the criminal is and it's time to make the arrest. Then you can watch 'The Diamond Robbery (Part 2)' to find out if you got the right man.

6 Working with graphics

In this module you will use a range of ICT skills and knowledge to:

> **Understand the use of graphics in ICT**
> **Consider how graphics can be used to inform, persuade and entertain**
> **Consider different methods of creating graphics**
> **Design and create your own graphics**
> **Use your own graphics**

Introduction

In this module you will be using ICT to create your own graphics. Graphics is the general name given to any type of picture or image that you might use in ICT. You have already used graphics a lot in InteraCT 1 and 2. For example:

> Adding clipart to your presentations and documents.
> Inserting digital photographs into web pages.
> Using WordArt to create effects with letters.
> Creating charts when using a spreadsheet.
> Creating flowcharts to show how control systems work.

Using graphics

Graphics can be used to inform the audience. They can help your audience understand what you are trying to tell them. For example, if you were trying to explain what a microlight was, it could be quite difficult to explain in words. If you show someone a picture they understand straight away.

A microlight is a flying machine that looks a bit like a hang-glider but has a compartment where the pilot sits and an engine – or you could show them the picture!

Graphics are also used to improve presentation. Graphics are used everywhere:

> On websites
> In documents
> In presentations
> In adverts
> On products

Figure 6.1 Microlight

Compare the two websites below. Which one looks the best? Which has the biggest impact on you?

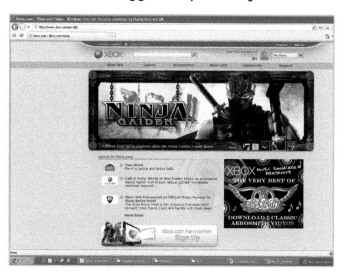

Figure 6.2 Xbox.com

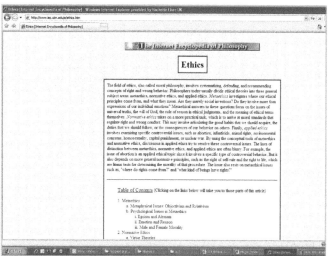

Figure 6.3 The Internet Encyclopedia of Philosophy

Compare the two products below: Tesco's Own Brand Organic and Tesco Value eggs. Which has the biggest visual impact?

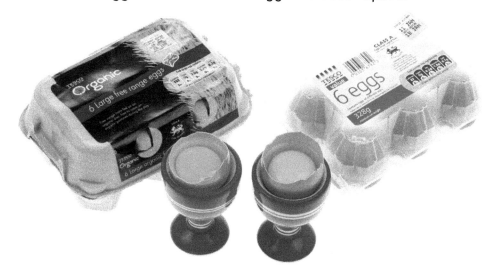

Figure 6.4 Packaging design

In this case one of the ways that graphics have been used is to create a logo. Logos are a clever use of graphics because people recognise them instantly even if there is no text. Here are some logos that don't use the name of the product but most people recognise them straight away.

Figure 6.5 Nike

Figure 6.6 Apple

The logo is a registered trademark of Daimler AG and is reproduced with the kind permission of Daimler AG/Photo © Mediacolor's/Alamy

Figure 6.7 Mercedes

Figure 6.8 PlayStation

Many companies use graphics to create mascots that people link with their products. Do you recognise these mascots and what products they are linked to?

Figure 6.9 Mascots for breakfast cereals

In this case the graphics are being used to entertain the audience and to persuade them to buy the product.

Creating graphics

There are many different ways of creating and editing graphics depending on what type of graphics you are using. For example, the software you might use to create logos and mascots would be different to that you use to work with photographs.

In this module we will be looking at the drawing tools available in Microsoft software such as Microsoft Word and Microsoft PowerPoint. If you have got specialist drawing software such as CorelDraw, SerifDraw, PaintShop Pro or Fireworks then it is better to use these as they have more features. You can also get software that allows you to create animated (moving) graphics, which can add even more impact to your presentations.

Once you have created your graphics you need to use them in your documents and presentations. The assignment for this module concerns your school. You are going to create a new logo and possibly a mascot to represent your school. You are then going to use the logo and mascot in some form of presentation.

 **Skills Tutorial 1**   This tutorial shows you how to create simple graphics using the drawing tools in Microsoft Word.

 Practical Task: Designing a logo and mascot

You need to think carefully about what kind of image you want to portray and how and where the logo and mascot will be used. Open the 'Designing a logo and mascot' worksheet on the website and follow the instructions.

 Practical Task: Using your logo and mascot

You now need to create some form of presentation using the logo and mascot. Open the 'Using your logo and mascot' worksheet on the website and follow the instructions.

6| SKILLS TUTORIAL 1

This tutorial will show you how to create simple graphics using the drawing tools in Microsoft Word. The same drawing tools are available in other Microsoft software such as Microsoft PowerPoint and Microsoft Publisher.

Figure 6.10 The Q Ball logo

As an example, we will be creating 'The Q Ball' logo that you saw in the presentation about the snooker hall. Here it is to remind you.

This is a fairly simple example using a coloured shape, some black text and some white text.

To create a shape:

- Open Microsoft Word.
- Select 'View' from the menus and make sure that the Drawing Toolbar is ticked.

The drawing toolbar is usually displayed at the bottom of the screen, as shown:

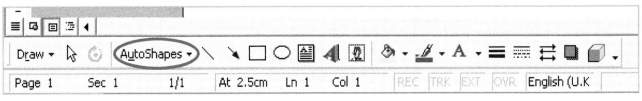

Figure 6.11 The drawing toolbar

To draw a shape:

- Click on the shape that you want to draw.

You will see an icon for the circle and the square. If you wanted a more unusual shape you can click on 'Autoshapes' and select from the list.

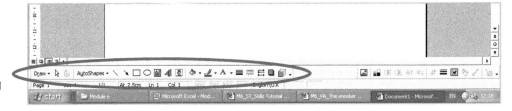

Figure 6.12 Autoshapes

- Click on the circle.
- Move the cursor into your document. You will notice that the mouse pointer shows as a small cross.

- Left click and hold to drag out the circle shape.
- You can move the mouse to make it bigger and smaller, and to change the shape between a circle and an oval.
- When you have got the shape and size you want, release the left mouse button.

You can see the outline of the shape that you will get. You can pick up and move this shape to re-size it at any time. It is just like any other graphic that you might use, for example clipart.

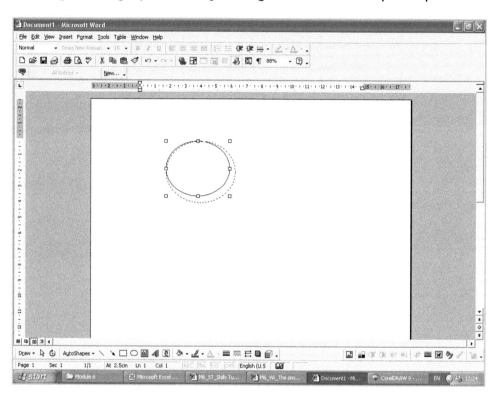

Figure 6.13 Re-sizing the circle

To change the colour of the circle:

- Right-click on the shape.
- Select 'Format AutoShape' and this screen will be displayed:

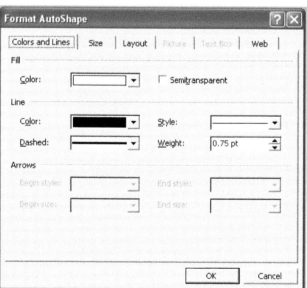

Figure 6.14 Changing the colour

69

You can now change the 'Fill' colour and the 'Line' colour by clicking on the little drop-down lists and selecting the colour. In this case we want the fill and line colour to be red. This creates the effect of having a red ball. You can experiment with the other options too.

To get the white 'Q' in the middle of the ball we need to add a text box and layer it on top of the ball. To do this:

● Click on the text box icon on the drawing toolbar:

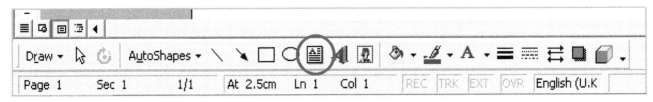

Figure 6.15 Text box icon

● Left-click over the red circle and drag out a text box roughly the right size.

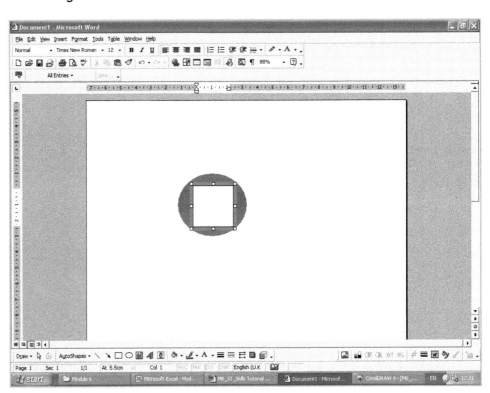

Figure 6.16 Adding a text box

- Now type in the letter Q, selecting the appropriate font style and size. In this case we have Arial Black size 72.
- You may need to make the text box bigger and reposition it in the centre of the circle.

You will notice that the text box has a black border and a white background that is covering up the red of the ball.

- Right click on the text box and select 'Format textbox'.
- Change the line colour to 'No line' using the drop-down list.
- Change the fill colour to 'No fill' using the drop-down list.
- Now highlight the letter Q and change the font colour to white.

All you need to do now is add two further text boxes, one for the word 'The' and one for the word 'Ball', and position them either side of the ball to create the logo.

Two other useful options when creating graphics like this is the use of 'Order' and 'Group', which you may have seen before.

Order is useful as it tells the computer in what order to show the graphics. For example if we had two balls overlapping each other we could use order to put one on top of the other.

If we added a blue ball and overlapped it slightly with the red one we have already created, the blue ball would automatically go on top:

Figure 6.17 Ordering the two balls

Skills Tutorial 1

To move the blue ball behind the red ball:

● Right-click on the blue ball.
● Select 'Order'.
● Select 'Send to Back'.

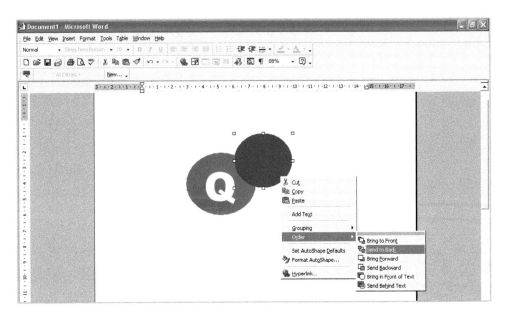

Figure 6.18 Moving back the blue ball

The blue ball will now be behind the red ball, as shown here:

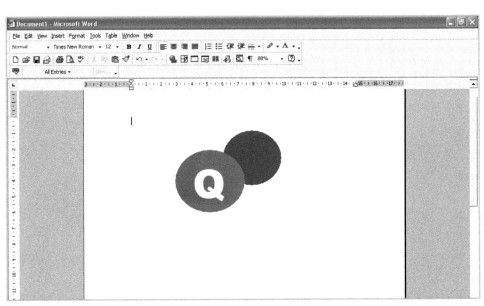

Figure 6.19 Red ball on top

The Group option is really useful when you have finished your design. At the moment your graphic is made up of several different shapes and text boxes. If you move one of these, it will mess it up. What you can do is group all the shapes and text boxes together so that they become one single graphic.

To do this:

● Click on the white arrow in the drawing toolbar.

Figure 6.20 Group icon

● Now left-click and drag a box around all the shapes and text boxes in your graphic.

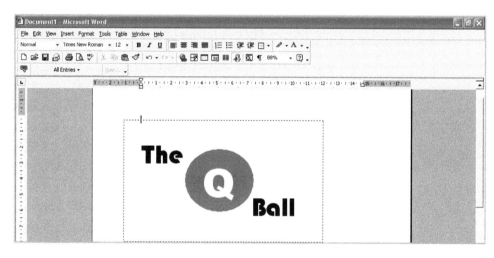

Figure 6.21 Creating a group

● Release the mouse button and right click.
● Select 'Grouping' and 'Group'.

You will see that this makes it into a single graphic that you can move around and re-size, just like a piece of clipart or a photograph.

● If you ever need to ungroup it, just right click and select 'Grouping' and 'Ungroup'.

Using these techniques you can create a range of different graphic effects. You can experiment with the various shapes, the use of different shading effects and overlaps to create different graphics. You will also see that you can add lines, and there is a freehand drawing tool too.

7 Creating a wiki

Learning Objectives	In this module you will use a range of ICT skills and knowledge to:

> **Analyse and evaluate information**
> **Consider plausibility, accuracy and bias of information**
> **Work together to collect information**
> **Work together to create an effective wiki**
> **Evaluate and make changes to a wiki based on your own and other people's observations**

Introduction

In this module you will be using ICT to create a wiki. A wiki is a type of website where the information on the site is put there by anyone who wants to put it there. Anyone is then allowed to add to and edit the information. This is sometime called a 'collaborative' website because lots of people contribute to it.

Wikis can be used for anything, but the most common use is as an encyclopaedia, which is a collection of information or knowledge. Some wikis, such as Wikipedia, contain information about all aspects of life. Others, such as Wikibooks, contain information on a specific topic (in this case, textbooks).

How do they work?

A wiki is just like any other website. It is made up of multimedia content such as text, graphics, photos, videos and sound. They tend to be quite plain in their layout though, as they contain quite a lot of text. Here's a typical page from Wikipedia:

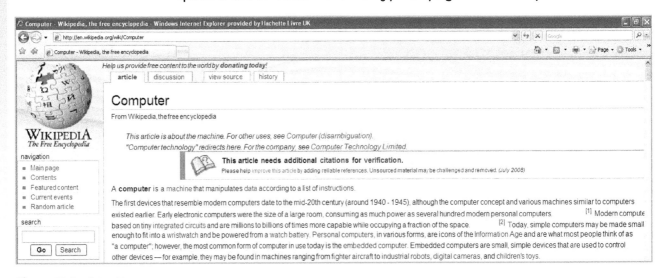

Figure 7.1 Wikipedia

Like other websites there are many links from one page to others. You can see them here highlighted in blue. Every time someone adds or changes something on a wiki, they can create links to other related topics. For example, if you were writing about the history of computing and mentioned the 'microchip', then you could create a link to the page that contains more detailed information on the microchip.

Can you trust a wiki?

There are thousands of wikis on the Internet. Some of them ask you to register before you can use them but many are open to everyone. This is one of the biggest problems with them. Anyone can read them and anyone can edit them. The information they put on the wiki might be fact or it might be opinion. In turn, another person can then come along and make changes to their changes. And on it goes.

Databases

Wikis also involve another strand of ICT – the use of databases. A database is a collection of information on a related topic. Many wikis link to large databases where all the information is stored. The wiki then uses web pages to display the information held in the database to make it easier for people to use.

All wikis have a search option. This works in the same way as an Internet search engine or the search or filter options that you have used in spreadsheet or database software. You type in your search words and it finds information related to your search.

Creating your own wiki

Anyone can create a wiki and that is what you are going to do next. You need more than one person to create a proper wiki so you will be working in groups to create a wiki on a topic of your choice. Later you will let the rest of the class loose on your wiki.

Updating the wiki

Your wiki is now complete but that is not the end of the story. In fact, what you have just created is only the start. People can now view what you have written and make any changes they like.

Fans of wikis argue that it is not possible for someone to get away with putting a biased view on them as, with so many people adding to them, someone else will change it. Critics of wikis think that the information is unreliable because you don't know who put it on the wiki or why.

Some wikis have 'moderators' who are trusted people who go through and check the changes that other people make. If the changes are wrong, they can change it back and even ban people from using the wiki.

Practical Task:
The history of computers
Open 'The History of computers' worksheet on the website and follow the instructions.

Practical Task:
Creating a wiki
Open the 'Creating a wiki' worksheet on the website and follow the instructions.

Practical Task:
Updating a wiki
Open the 'Updating a wiki' worksheet on the website and follow the instructions.

8 Security systems

Learning Objectives	In this module you will use a range of ICT skills and knowledge to:

> Create sequences of instructions or flowcharts to control events
> Test your flowcharts to make sure they are precise and efficient
> Create a complete security system
> Use a spreadsheet simulation to test a security system
> Suggest and make changes to a spreadsheet simulation

Introduction

In this module you will use ICT to create a security control system for a top-secret research centre. You will be looking at the ways in which ICT systems and devices can be used to stop unauthorised people getting access to the building.

You will need to think about how an intruder might break into the building and how you can stop them. You will also be asked to put the security system to the test to see if it is possible for someone to break it.

Figure 8.1 Security guard

Background

The Connolly Centre carries out top-secret research for the government. The building itself is located in the middle of the Scottish countryside.

A plan of the building and grounds is shown on the next page. Notice that a perimeter fence surrounds the whole building and that there is only one entrance to the site. There is just one building, which has a main entrance and a fire exit. There are no windows.

You can see that there are a number of rooms. Notice the room marked in red: this is the most important room in the building as it is where the main computer server is located.

Twenty five people work at the centre. They have to go through various security checks every time they enter or leave the centre.

Setting up a control system

The centre has one security guard who sits just inside the main entrance to the building. The Government are relying on you to put a security control system in place that will alert the guard if anyone tries to break in.

Figure 8.2 Plan of the Connolly Centre

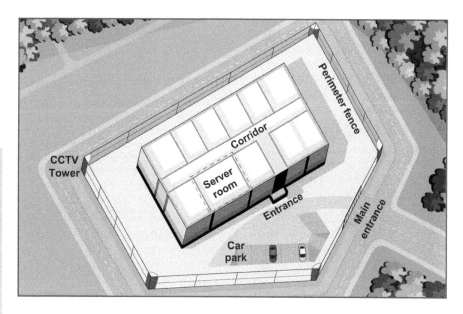

 Practical Task:
Security control

Open the 'Security control' document on the website and follow the instructions.

You have got as much money as you need and you can choose whatever devices you want to make the centre secure.

Testing the control system

The server room is the most important room in the building and the Government wants it to have extra protection. The biggest danger is at night as, if someone manages to break into the building, there will be no one around to see them.

They have a plan to keep the room safe and they want you to test it. They have created a model of the room using a spreadsheet. They have put various sensors in the room to detect intruders.

Figure 8.3 Spreadsheet model for the server room

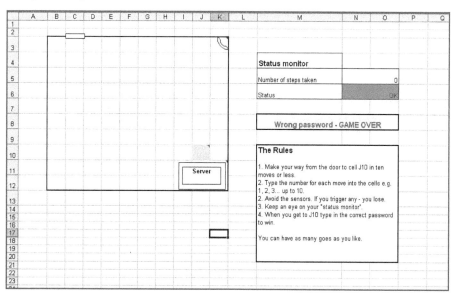

 Practical Task:
Security simulation

Open the 'Security simulation' document on the website and follow the instructions.

It's time for your next task, which is to see whether you can break through the security and to see whether you can suggest a better system.

CHALLENGES

·············· Challenge 1 – Shopping habits

Figure 1 Electronics retailer

You have been asked by a large electronics retailer to carry out research into the shopping habits of young people and then report back on what you have found out.

The research could include finding out the following information:

> What are the main things that young people spend their money on?
> How much shopping is done online compared to in shops?
> How much money do young people spend in an average week?
> Do girls spend more than boys?
> Where do young people get their money from and how much do they get?

You can present your findings in whatever way you think is most suitable. You may choose more than one method of presenting the results.

·············· Challenge 2 – Census data

Figure 2 Census data in your local area

Your challenge is to analyse changes in your local area based on Census data so that you could explain it to a friend. The census is usually undertaken every 10 years and has been since 1801. The last census was in 2001 and the next one is due in 2011. In England and Wales, the census is carried out by the Office for National Statistics. In Scotland it is the General Register Office for Scotland and in Northern Ireland it is the Northern Ireland Statistics and Research Agency.

You can look into any part of the census data and try and answer questions such as:

> How has housing changed since 2001?
> Do people still do the same kind of work that they did years ago?
> Do people live longer now than they did many years ago?
> Has the population increased or decreased in the area?
> Do people have a better standard of living now compared to many years ago?

Challenge 3 – Family tree

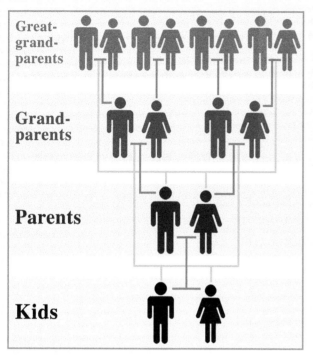

Figure 3 Family tree

Your challenge is to create a family tree that you could present as a gift to a member of your own family. You should start with yourself at the bottom and then work your way up as far as you can go. You should try and go back as far as possible into your family history.

You will need to collect the information from wherever you can get it. Initially this may be from your family members. To trace your family back even further you may use government records that are available from your library or over the Internet.

You can present the information in whatever way you think is most suitable. As this is being designed as a gift, you may choose to use multimedia tools such as photographs or even video.

Challenge 4 – Soap opera

Figure 4 Scene from *Coronation Street*

Your challenge is to write, record and produce a 'pilot episode' of your own soap opera. Your soap opera can be set anywhere you like but you must create an original dramatic piece of work that would make people want to tune in and watch or listen to it again.

Many TV shows start with a pilot episode that introduces the main characters, locations and plot lines. If the viewers or listeners like the pilot episode then a whole show will get commissioned so it is important that your show has a good impact.

The main steps are:

> Decide on the location, characters and main plot lines
> Write a script that includes directing instructions as well as the actual words that your actors will speak
> Record your soap opera
> Edit it and finalise it ready for the viewers/listeners.

Challenge 5 – Video conferencing

Figure 5 Video conference

Your challenge is to communicate with students from another school using video conferencing (or webcams). When you have achieved this you should write a report that describes the issues you had to deal with using the software.

The main steps in this challenge are:

> Identify and set up the hardware that you will need
> Identify what software you want to use
> Find someone from another school who you can make contact with
> Communicate with the other school using the technology
> Write a report explaining how you did it, including any problems you faced

Challenge 6 – Historical bias

Figure 6 Fidel Castro

Your challenge is to select a famous and controversial person from history and to find different accounts of their impact on society. For example, Fidel Castro is seen as a dictator by some people but as a charismatic leader by others.

The main steps here are:

> Try to find information from all sides of the argument
> Double or triple-check your information to ensure that you are presenting a balanced viewpoint
> Draw your own conclusions about the person
> Try to work out what information is fact and what is opinion, and present an unbiased conclusion

Challenge 7 – Business idea

Figure 7 Pitching a business idea

Your challenge is to come up with a new idea for a business. It might help to think of the *Dragons' Den* programme, where people 'pitch' their ideas to the dragons in the hope that they will put money into the business.

You need to:

> Come up with an idea for an imaginary product or service that you could offer
> Create a presentation that would persuade someone to invest in your business: your presentation should include images and explanations of the product or service that you are offering
> Ask someone to act as the 'dragon' so that your ideas really get tested

Challenge 8 – Historical event

Figure 8 The Dunkirk evacuations

Your challenge is to create two presentations that give opposing views of a major event in history. For example, the Dunkirk evacuations in 1940 were portrayed as a major victory by both sides. You can choose any event.

You need to:

> Select a suitable historical event
> Research and collect information that gives opposing views of the event
> Create two presentations
> Ensure that both presentations are factual and unbiased

Challenge 9 – Storyboard

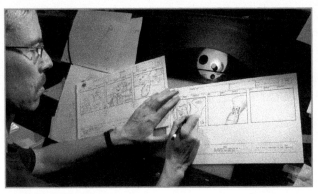

Figure 9 Cartoonist drawing a storyboard

Your challenge is to create a storyboard or comic strip covering a social issue of your choice. The idea of the storyboard is to tackle a difficult subject and produce a realistic story that could help someone who might be having problems. For example, you may choose a topic such as bullying, exam stress or peer pressure.

The main steps here are:

> Choose a suitable social issue
> Carry out some research into the issue and identify the main points that you want to tackle
> Produce your storyboard using either animation or a series of photographs

Challenge 10 – Interactive story

When he walked out of the barn, Jack saw a cow and a dog. "Which one should I follow?" he thought to himself.

Figure 10 Screen from an interactive story

Your challenge is to use ICT to produce an interactive story. This means that the reader will be able to take different routes at certain points within the story. You may give the reader options that lead to different outcomes.

You can present this in whatever form you like, for example:

> Create a Microsoft PowerPoint presentation or Microsoft Word document
> Write the first slide or page of the story
> Use hyperlinks to allow the reader to take different routes through the story
> Write other slides/pages as the story progresses, making sure that all the links work and that the story makes sense

Challenge 11 – Mash up

Figure 11 DJ at her decks

Your challenge is to create or download two music tracks and then to create a 'mash up' of the two tracks. A mash up typically takes the bass line and drum beat from one song and the melody from another to create a whole new track.

You may like to:

> Listen to some existing 'mash ups' to get the idea
> Use music software to write your own tracks
> Use midi keyboards or other instruments to record your own tracks
> Download copyright-free tracks and use them to mix together
> Use specialist music software designed to mix tracks together

Challenge 12 – Filing system

Figure 12 Shelves of CDs and DVDs

Your challenge is to create a computerised record of your entire music and film collection. You should record certain basic information about each track/film, such as the title, duration and location. This should cover both your computerised music/films and the ones you own on CD or DVD.

The purpose of setting up a system like this is to make it easy for you to find particular music/films when you need to. This should be set up so that you can easily search for a particular track or film using different search criteria. For example, you should be able to:

> Search your system for all of the comedy films that you own
> Search for all the music tracks within a particular genre, for example RnB
> Search for all films starring a particular actor
> Search for all tracks by a particular artist

When you have finished, analyse how suitable your solution is to the problem.

Challenge 13 – GCSE options

Figure 13 Students in the ICT suite

Your challenge is to create a computer system that would allow your teacher to analyse how many students are taking which GCSEs next year. Your system must be capable of producing basic reports and graphs for the teacher to analyse, and cover all subjects.

For example, your system should be able to:

> Let the teacher look at how many students have selected a particular subject (for example ICT) and then find out which students they are
> Produce a report to show how many students are doing each subject
> Produce a graph to show how many students are doing each subject

When you have finished, analyse how suitable your solution is to the problem.

Challenge 14 – Ring tone

Figure 14 Mobile phone

Your challenge is to create, record and upload a new ring tone to your phone.

You may do this:

> By downloading specialist software from the Internet
> By recording your own music using midi instruments
> By downloading music and converting it into the correct format for your mobile phone

Challenge 15 – Traffic predictor

Figure 15 Traffic on the road

Your challenge is to create a computer model that will predict the number and different types of vehicles that will pass the school in a 24-hour period. You need to base your predictions on a sample of data, which you will need to collect yourself. You need to take into account different times of the day and night, and what affect you think this will have on traffic flow.

Some questions you might ask yourself are:

> How many vehicles pass a particular point during a set period?
> Will this pattern be the same throughout the day or will it be busier/quieter at certain times?
> Can you estimate the volume of traffic at different times or do you need to take further samples?
> What type of vehicles are passing by?
> Does the type of vehicle vary with the time of day?

When you have finished write a brief report explaining how your model works. Explain whether you think your model is accurate and what you could do to make it more realistic.

Challenge 16 – Crowd size

Figure 16 Football stadium

Your challenge is to create a computer model that will predict how many people will be in the crowd at the next sporting event of your choice. This could be anything from your local football team to a school sports competition.

You need to think carefully about what factors will affect the size of the crowd. For example:

> What day of the week and time of day is the event on?
> How much does it cost?
> Is it easy to get to?
> What else is happening on that day?
> What is the weather forecast and will this affect how many people come along?

When you have finished, assess how accurate you think your model is and what you could do to make it more realistic.

INDEX